THE ELLIS ISLAND IMMIGRANT COOKBOOK

BY TOM BERNARDIN

"One of the year's more engaging cookbooks..."

THE NEW YORK TIMES

THANKS TO:

Pamela Blackwell, Tom Burgio, Claudia Carlson, Terry Crownfield, Jim Fobel, Maxine Gold, Lee Goodman, Mary Angela Hardwick, Bob Maitland, Max Makow, Don Mintz, Tanna Moontaro, Stephen Morgen, Barry Moreno, Sherry Ogur, Joshua Pentz, Philip Sceri, Peter Valentini and Peg Zitko.

Hello to my friends from the National Park Service.

To order, you can call 24 hours 1-800-362-2489. Major credit cards accepted.

Books are $16.95 each, $3.00 postage/handling. 3 or more books to same address, $2.00 p/h each. By mail: make checks payable to Richardson Specialties. Mail to P. O. Box 8030 Brik, NJ 08723. NJ residents please add applicable sales tax.

Library of Congress Card Catalog #: 91-91932

ISBN: 0-9629198-2-9

Copyright 1991 Tom Bernardin

Published by Tom Bernardin, Inc.
Suite 2306
175 Fifth Avenue
New York, New York 10010
(212) 229-0202

FIRST PRINTING NOVEMBER 1991

SECOND PRINTING MAY 1992

THIRD PRINTING MARCH 1993

FOURTH PRINTING OCOTBER 1994

BREAK, BREAK, BREAK

Break, break, break,
  On thy cold gray stones, O Sea!
And I would that my tongue could utter
  The thoughts that arise in me.

O well for the fisherman's boy,
  That he shouts with his sister at play!
O well for the sailor lad,
  That he sings in his boat on the bay!

And the stately ships go on
  To their haven under the hill;
But O for the touch of a vanished hand,
  And the sound of a voice that is still!

Break, break, break,
  At the foot of thy crags, O Sea!
But the tender grace of a day that is dead
  Will never come back to me.

Alfred, Lord Tennyson, 1842

"Food and history combine in Ellis Island Cookbook..."
SAN DIEGO UNION

"Cookbook tale of American dream..."
PALM BEACH POST

"Ellis Island Immigrant Cookbook provides glimpse into our culinary past..."
MIDDLESEX NEWS

"Taste of old country passed down in families..."
HARTFORD COURANT

"A treasury of recipes from the melting-pot cooks..."
THE NEWS-TIMES

"Immigrant cookbook makes history, culture come alive..."
THE INDEPENDENT

"What is valuable and a joy to read are the stories of the hopeful newcomers who passed through Ellis Island..."
THE DAY

"Familiar recipes arrived with immigrants at Ellis Island..."
NAPLES DAILY NEWS

"Immigrants preserved culture with foods..."
RECORD-JOURNAL

"A look at our immigrant past through Ellis Island recipes..."
FLORIDA TODAY

"Old world flavors are immigrants' legacy to descendants..."
SAINT PAUL PIONEER PRESS

"For over a century, America's immigrants cherished family recipes as link to homeland..."
LAWRENCE EAGLE TRIBUNE

"A history of immigrants through their recipes..."
THE SUN

TABLE OF CONTENTS

INTRODUCTION

It would be unfair to myself, the contributors to this book, and a very special friend if I didn't begin exactly where I wanted.

In 1972, on a very serendipitous and rainy November Saturday shortly after I arrived in New York, I found myself on a walking tour of cast-iron architecture given by a most remarkable woman, Margot Gayle. There, squeezed into a doorway on lower Broadway, I heard the history of New York unfold through its rich architectural heritage. She spoke so enthusiastically of the city's growth and history that as the gray day turned into a darker evening, I felt as if I had been transported to nineteenth-century New York. The cast-iron buildings, lampposts, and street clocks were from another world. She easily knew the importance of preserving our past and was most anxious for us to understand. I then joined Margot's organization, the Friends Of Cast-Iron Architecture. My membership card arrived attached to a small magnet to use in testing a building to see if it was made of iron. I was hooked !

I shortly became a volunteer and would often trek down to her West Ninth Street Greenwich Village apartment. We spent many hours typing and talking. It was, and is, a rich and rewarding experience just to be in her company. Soon we mounted a campaign to save thirty of the old bishop-crook lampposts that once lined the streets of Manhattan. At that time I was teaching English to recent immigrants to America but due to the fiscal crisis of 1976, found myself out of work. Margot knew I was a collector of Statue of Liberty memorabilia and suggested I try to find a job there. I was, and still am, so enamored of the Statue that it had never occurred to me that one could actually just go there and find a job. Within a few days I was interviewing for a position at the Statue and also for one at Ellis Island, both being part of The Statue of Liberty National Monument.

It was on another rainy cold day in April 1978 that I first went out to Ellis Island. That was several years before the restoration began and the buildings were in deplorable disrepair. Only a small part of the island was safe enough to take visitors through, and after a two-week orientation and education program, we started giving tours of this dramatic and wonderful place. I found myself becoming gradually more absorbed in the stories of the people who had come there so many years before. On days when no visitors came, we had the run of the island and we began to explore. I'm not sure I encountered any ghosts, but certainly the deserted island and the buildings were filled with an overwhelming sense of importance and drama. Being part of its history and sharing it with wonderful co-workers and friends was certainly more than I could ever have hoped for. I returned for two more seasons, leaving shortly before Ellis closed once again, this time to begin restoration.

It was not so easy to walk away from such a profound experience, and soon I developed a slide-lecture program entitled "Ellis Island - The Golden Door." I presented over fifty of these programs, mostly to senior-citizen groups and nursing homes. Many of these people I was now meeting had been processed at Ellis at the beginning of their lives, and they were thrilled to know that their deep courage was being recognized by the people of America. Their "Plymouth Rock" was being saved for future generations, for all of us to try and learn of their extraordinary saga.

In giving tours of Ellis and talking with the immigrants, I became aware of how important food was to their experience, not just on a nutritional level, but as a means of bringing with them, and preserving, this part of their earlier lives. Soon they would shed their old clothes, learn to speak some English and, reluctantly or not, become Americanized. But their love for their foods from the old country was something they could not and, thankfully, did not give up. The rich smells from their kitchens surely brought a deep nostalgia for people and places they had left behind.

A couple of years later I did a national recipe search. This was a new experience for me and I had no idea what to expect. Well, once again Ellis Island has brought me a heartening experience. The generosity and encouragement of the responses were beyond my wildest expectations. Some of the recipes I received were from the immigrants themselves, but most were from their children and grandchildren. Many, if not most, were very anxious to share that part of their lives that was so deeply affected by their immigrant ancestors. Indeed, some of the letters read like love letters to the past they remember so well through the smells and memories of sharing foods they loved. I know for myself that all I have to do is make some Boston Baked Beans, and the smell alone transports me to Lawrence, Massachusetts, and the five of us laughing, joking, and teasing, with our parents desperately trying to maintain order.

My sincerest thanks go to all of you who were so kind to share your memories with me. And, of course, to my special friend, Margot Gayle. Thank you all.

Tom Bernardin

THE STORY OF ELLIS ISLAND

The story of Ellis Island begins on the southern tip of Manhattan within Battery Park at Castle Clinton. Built originally as a fort in 1808, it eventually became a concert hall known as Castle Garden. From 1855 to 1890 Castle Garden served as the primary immigration processing station in the United States. (Many immigrants would remember it as "kesslegarten.") During those years, 8,000,000 immigrants were processed there. As the tide of immigration increased, it became apparent that the facilities at Castle Garden were inadequate to handle the many problems the immigrants presented. The overcrowding became intolerable, while corruption was rampant, with thieves descending upon the unsuspecting immigrants. When the federal government took responsibility for the processing in 1890, officials looked for alternative sites. They didn't have to look far because located in New York Harbor, between Battery Park and New Jersey, lay a three-acre oyster bed, called Ellis Island. It was named after an eighteenth-century owner, Samuel Ellis, a New Jersey farmer. Prior to that it was named Kioshk (or Gull) Island by the Native Americans who would frequent it for the oysters. On eighteenth-century maps it was called Oyster Island, Bucking Island and later Gibbet Island. The officials hoped that by moving the place of inspection to an island they would have more control over the treatment of the immigrants.

Main building at Ellis Island. The first wooden structure was replaced with this building in 1900.

Measuring 400' by 150' and made of Georgia pine, the building opened on January 1, 1892. (Between 1890, when Castle Garden closed, and 1892, when Ellis opened, the Barge Office in Battery Park was used for receiving immigrants.) Unfortunately, five years later, on June 14, 1897, a fire broke out, destroying the entire complex. The two hundred immigrants on the island were all taken to safety and the Barge Office was again put into service until a new facility could be built.

At the time of construction of the present-day structure, America was in a depression and immigration statistics led officials to believe that the days of mass immigration were over. How wrong they were! Built to receive no more than 500,000 new immigrants a year, it was soon swarmed with prospective citizens. Steamship companies, eager to make a sale, placed posters throughout Europe with pictures of cornucopias to entice would-be immigrants. News that there was work in America spread quickly through Europe and many who saw no prospect of a better life at home decided to try and see what this new, young land had to offer. With immigrants numbering over 5,000 a day, the facilities were far too small. Construction began again and ultimately a total of thirty-three buildings were built, including dormitories, hospitals, contagious disease wards, and dining rooms. At peak times there were more than 500 people working at Ellis, including inspectors, interpreters, doctors, nurses, matrons, clerks. Many worked twelve-hour days, seven days a week. Ellis Island was virtually a city unto itself.

After a long and arduous journey to America, the steamships would arrive in New York Harbor. Medical inspectors would board the ship and give a cursory examination to the first- and second-class passengers. They felt that if one had the money for an expensive ticket, he or she would be unlikely to become a public charge, one of the main reasons for the inspection process at Ellis. The steamships then berthed in the many piers that once lined New York waters. Those first- and second-class passengers were free to go on to their new lives in America, while steerage class passengers were grouped, tagged and put on piers to await transportation to Ellis. Steamship companies were required to keep strict manifests which included detailed information on each immigrant, including name, age, occupation and former address. These manifests would later be given to immigration officials at Ellis Island as the basis for the legal inspection. In an effort to create some order out of such chaos, tags were placed on the immigrants to keep those on the same manifest page together.

Travelling steerage class was no doubt an experience most were anxious to forget. The average trans-Atlantic voyage lasted from eight to fifteen days. Steerage-class tickets cost approximately thirty dollars. Many had saved for years to be able to afford the tickets for an entire family.

Double and triple bunk beds, minimal facilities and horrible food must have made many immigrants wish they had never left home. Oftentimes, steerage class passengers were allowed on deck for only a brief time each day. By the time they arrived many were no doubt sick, exhausted and frightened.

Steerage passengers aboard the *Westernland*, 1901. This scene is in sharp contrast to the illustrations steamship companies posted in Europe to entice would-be immigrants.

Immigrants arriving at Ellis Island.

Once at Ellis Island, the immigrants were met by inspectors who rapidly directed them under a large canopy and into the baggage room. In satchels swung over their shoulders or, if they were from a larger city, in a wicker basket, they would have placed what they felt they needed to begin their new lives: a Bible, family photograph, some clothing, perhaps a samovar and most important of all, a perene, a down-filled comforter which often became part of a woman's dowry. Uniformed inspectors would try to get the immigrants to check their bags; however, many of the immigrants were afraid of uniforms and besides, could they trust these Americans with all their worldly belongings? However, there was another reason for the immigrants to carry their bags as they were being processed. They all knew that they were about to undergo a medical examination and a bag could be used to disguise a limp. The inspectors were there to make sure that the immigrants would be able to work; any physical problem could be grounds for denying admittance. From the baggage room they were directed up a flight of stairs which led to the Registry Room, also known as the Great Hall. Unknown to the immigrants as they climbed the stairs, their medical examination had begun. At the top of the stairs were two inspectors observing the immigrants. They were watching to see who had difficulty making the climb.

With chalk marks hastily written on the immigrant's lapel, the inspectors would indicate any potential problems. An "H" would warn of a heart problem, an "L" of lameness. Upon entering this enormous room, surely the largest they would have ever seen, they were confronted by a system of walkways called "cattleruns." As the immigrant walked the passageway, he would encounter different inspectors. One would check limbs and fingers; another would check hair and scalp. The most feared was the "eye" man. At that time trachoma was a very contagious eye disease. Incurable, it would require that the immigrant be returned to the port of departure. The inspector would place a buttonhook under the immigrant's eyelid and check for any signs of redness. If there were any indications of the disease, he would take his chalk, mark an "E" to indicate a problem and the immigrant would be put aside for further examination.

Registry Hall, Ellis Island, circa 1911.

Most of the immigrants, however, did not have medical problems and within a few hours they would find themselves at the other end of the hall waiting for the legal examination. There was a row of tall legal desks, behind each a legal inspector and beside him an interpreter. It was their responsibility to make sure the immigrant had no legal reasons to deny him entry. With the immigrants arriving daily in such numbers, it was impossible for the inspectors to spend too much time on each immigrant. They had about two minutes to ask a series of twenty-nine questions: "What is your name? Where do you come from? Why did you come here? Do you have any money? Do you have any relatives in America? Are you an anarchist?" Perhaps the most important question of all was, "Do you have a job waiting for you?" The unions were just developing at that time and it was illegal for an employer to import labor. Those immigrants who answered "Yes" were forced to go before a Board Of Special Inquiry, where they were given an opportunity to plead their cases. Most immigrants, however, were prepared for these questions. It was the steamship's responsibility to return any immigrant denied entry to the port of departure. Therefore, they had coached the immigrants as to the correct answers to give. It was, basically, up to the immigrant to show an ability to work and a desire to do so. Most accomplished this within five hours. About twenty percent of the immigrants were detained: some for only one night as they waited for a relative to appear, or possibly for a longer time, waiting for a medical problem to clear up. It must be remembered that only 2% of those coming here were forced to return. That is a small figure in some ways, but in human terms it translates to about 250,000 people whose lives were surely marked by deep disappointment.

Looking for signs of trachoma during the eye examination at Ellis Island.

The Money Exchange

After their inspection, immigrants could change their foreign currency into U. S. dollars at the money exchange on the island. They could then purchase railroad tickets to their final destination. The concessions at Ellis Island were held by private contractors and required constant vigilance by the immigration officials on the island to assure provision of decent and honest service.

The immigration service provided immigrants with free postcards to notify friends or relatives in the U. S. of their arrival. After years of separation many families were reunited on Ellis Island at a spot popularly known as "the Kissing Post of America."

At the end of five hours, one-third of the immigrants were given a pass to board the "Ellis Island" ferry to take them to Manhattan. The other two-thirds traveled by barges which were pulled to New Jersey to make train connections for points across the United States.

The immigrants were not without friends at Ellis Island. An important part of the story is the contribution of the many and various social service agencies such as the Hebrew Immigrant Aid Society, The Italian Welfare League, the Red Cross, the YWCA, The National Council of Jewish Women, and the Daughters of the American Revolution. These volunteers were there to assist the immigrants in finding employment, a lost relative, or simply providing a kind word or shoulder to cry on.

With so many people bringing such large expectations to Ellis Island it must have been a place of heartbreaking sorrow. Families were forced to make hasty decisions when forced to separate. Who would stay with a sick child or accompany an immigrant denied entry back home? Assurances were made to send money back to the old country so that family members following later would be able to enter second class, thereby avoiding Ellis Island altogether. To those who were denied entry it surely earned its name as *The Island Of Tears*, *Isola delle Lacrime* to the Italians, and *Tranen Insel* to the Germans.

Volunteers from *The National Council of Jewish Women* (left) assisting Russian-Jewish women (center) in 1906.

The Rooftop Playground at Ellis Island. As immigration decreased, it was possible for the government to provide more amenities for those detained.

Those who truly believed that the streets were "paved with gold" were surely in for a rude awakening. What they did find, however, was a country that had coal to be mined, canals and subways to be dug, fields to till and factories to man. For this, America promised the chance for a dignified wage, the freedom to worship as one pleased, and a future for their children: in short, a piece of the American Dream.

This *Golden Door*, situated in the shadow of the Statue of Liberty, has come to represent the best of what America had to offer: a chance to begin again. Our lives are the products of their dreams and courage. We must always hold that sacred.

THE *ELLIS ISLAND* FERRY

Sadly, one of the most important artifacts from the days of mass immigration is lost to us forever. The *Ellis Island* ferry served for over fifty years, carrying the New York-bound immigrants to Manhattan. It was built in 1904 and had its last run on November 29, 1954.

During those years, it carried about 15,000,000 passengers and logged about 1,000,000 nautical miles. Measuring 144' by 45', it had two decks. The lower held 1,000 immigrants and the upper carried officials and visitors from New York.

After Ellis Island closed, the ferry was decommissioned and docked in the slip at Ellis. Unfortunately, on August 10, 1968, it sank. Efforts to salvage it as part of the restoration of Ellis Island proved futile. When the Navy recently tried to raise the boat, they discovered it covered with 500 tons of mud.

CHRONOLOGY

1600's   A 3.3-acre sandbank surrounded by oyster beds is called Kioshk, meaning Gull Island, by Native Americans.

1628   Known as one of the Oyster Islands by settlers, the island becomes a favorite fishing spot for the Dutch.

1680   The island is owned by William Dyre and is called Dyre's Island.

1765   After a pirate is hanged there, the island is nicknamed Gibbet Island.

1785   By this date, ownership of the island has come into the hands of Samuel Ellis.

1808   The Federal Government purchases Ellis Island for $10,000.00 from New York State, which had acquired it from the family of Samuel Ellis.

1812   Fort Gibson is constructed on Ellis Island as the federal government increases fortification of New York Harbor. Other forts included Castle Williams on Governors Island, Castle Clinton on the Battery and Fort Wood on Bedloe's (now Liberty) Island.

1850   On September 11, Jenny Lind, The Swedish Nightingale, appears at Castle Garden before a crowd of 10,000.

1855-90   Castle Garden becomes the first immigration inspection station in the U.S. Administered by New York State, in those thirty-five years 8,000,000 immigrants would be inspected there.

1875   First federal immigration legislation bars convicts, prostitutes and Chinese contract laborers from entering the United States.

1882   Those immigrants "likely to become a public charge" are excluded from entry. Chinese immigration is curtailed.

1885   Congress passes Alien Contract Labor Law which prohibits companies from importing labor from abroad.

1890   Castle Garden closes. The Federal Government assumes responsibility for immigration. Construction begins at Ellis Island on a receiving station made of Georgia pine.

1890-92 While Ellis Island is under construction, the Barge office (site of the present-day Coast Guard Station in Battery Park) is used to process immigrants.

1891   Paupers, polygamists, the insane, and persons with "loathsome or dangerous contagious diseases" are excluded from entry to the United States.

1892   January 1, the first immigrant to arrive at Ellis Island is Annie Moore from County Cork, Ireland.

1897   June 14 fire destroys the Ellis Island facility. All 200 immigrants are safely evacuated with no casualties. All of the immigration records dating from 1890 and some from Castle Garden are destroyed.

         Boring and Tilton are awarded contract to design a new fireproof immigration depot. Their limestone and brick building is the first constructed under the Tarsney Act, requiring competitive bidding for governmental structures.

1900   On December 17, Ellis Island reopens. The new facility includes the main building with its impressive Registry Room which becomes known as the "Great Hall."

1903   Iron and glass canopy constructed as a shelter for arriving immigrants. In 1933 this canopy is removed. A similar canopy is erected during the 1980's restoration.

            Steamship companies are now required to pay $100.00 penalty for each immigrant refused entry to the United States.

            Anarchists are prohibited from immigrating to the U.S.

1904   A children's playground is installed on the roof of the main building.

1907   April 17 is Ellis Island's busiest day with 11,745 immigrant arrivals.

            In 1907 over one million immigrants are processed; 195,540 immigrants are detained.

1911   The north-west wing of the third story of the main building is completed. Wooden benches are placed in the Registry Room to replace the "cattle runs".

            13,000 or 2% of all arriving immigrants are refused entry to the United States and are returned to their ports of embarkation.

1917   Literacy test required for all immigrants over 16 years of age. The Gustavino ceiling is installed in the Registry Room after the original ceiling was damaged in 1916 by an explosion at the Black Tom Wharf, a nearby New Jersey pier.

            Almost all immigration from Asia is banned.

1918   US Army and Navy take over Ellis Island. Registry Room is used as a hospital ward. Medical inspection of all immigrants now takes place on board steamships (until 1920).

1917-1919   Ellis Island serves as a detention center for enemy aliens, a way station for Navy personnel, and a hospital for the Army and Navy.

1919-54   Ellis Island serves as a deportation center and an immigration station.

1921   The Quota Act of 1921 is passed. This temporary law restricts immigration by limiting admission of each nationality to 3% of its number in the 1910 U. S. census. Immigration from eastern and southern Europe is sharply reduced. This law and the introduction of quotas signal the end of mass immigration to the United States.

1924   The Immigration Act of 1924 permanently restricts the number of immigrants from each country to 2% of the population of that nationality living in the United States in 1890. Immigrants are now inspected in countries of origin.

1927   The total U. S. immigration quota is now limited to about 150,000.

1933   The iron and glass canopy is removed. The WPA makes this and other changes, including final building construction on the island.

1954   On November 29, Ellis Island closes.

1965   Ellis Island becomes part of the Statue of Liberty National Monument by proclamation of President Lyndon Johnson.

1976   Ellis Island reopens for limited visitation.

1984   Ellis Island closes for total restoration of the main building.

1990   The Ellis Island Immigration Museum opens.

FOOD AT ELLIS ISLAND

When the federal government took over the responsibility of inspecting the immigrants in 1890, the idea of moving the inspection process to an island was attractive to the officials. Castle Garden, located on the mainland, provided too easy a target for the thieves and criminals that would prey upon the unsuspecting immigrants. In addition, by the time Castle Garden closed, the corruption within the inspection process was bordering on a public scandal. The concession contracts were often awarded by patronage, not for the quality of the services they offered the immigrants. Officials hoped for a clean sweep of those mistreating the immigrants.

On the steamships, passengers were provided with little to eat in steerage except lukewarm soups, black bread, boiled potatoes, herring or stringy beef. In the early years, any hopes the immigrants had in receiving better treatment at Ellis Island were futile. It did not take long for corruption to find its way to Ellis Island. Surely the first concessionaire made himself a rich man at the expense of the immigrants' stomachs. The detained immigrants were generally served stewed prunes over dried bread. Often there was no cutlery. Bowls were used and reused without washing; floors and tables often went unwashed. When they were washed, it was often by an intimidated immigrant.

As time went on, the commissioners became more involved in the treatment of the immigrants and the situation improved. Food, including thick soups and stews, became plentiful. The facilities were better maintained and, in time, ethnic and kosher meals were provided. This both solved and created problems. An immigrant appearing at the wrong seating might be exposed to unfamiliar foods. White bread was thought to be cake; bananas were a complete enigma. How strange and frightening it must have been!

As most of the immigrants were not detained and were destined for points outside New York City, provisions were made to supply them with some food for their train trips. Boxes of food, fifty cents for a small one and one dollar for a large one, were sold to the immigrants in the railroad waiting room. The contents of each box were printed on the sides, with corresponding prices, in several languages: two pounds of bread, eight cents; one pound cervelat sausage, twenty-two cents; five sandwiches, twenty cents; four pies, twenty cents; two boxes of cake, twenty cents; oranges or apples, ten cents. Surely the immigrants wasted no time in tasting the contents of the boxes to sample the flavors of their new country.

Mealtimes were one of the few times the detained immigrants were reunited with family members. Surely the enormity of their decision to come to America was hammered home when they sat down to eat and did not know what they were eating, or how they were to eat it. No doubt they were most anxious to recreate the comforting smells of the kitchens they had left behind.

BILLS OF FARE FOR ELLIS ISLAND
DINING ROOM

NOVEMBER 19, 1906

BREAKFAST

Coffee with Milk and Sugar
Bread and Butter
Crackers and Milk for
Women and Children

DINNER

Beef Stew
Boiled Potatoes and Rye Bread
Smoked or Pickled
Herring for the Hebrews
Crackers and Milk for
Women and Children

SUPPER

Baked Beans
Stewed Prunes and Rye Bread
Tea with Milk and Sugar
Crackers and Milk for
Women and Children

SUNDAY, JULY 1, 1917

BREAKFAST

Rice with Milk and Sugar
Served in Soup Plates
Stewed Prunes
Bread and Butter
Coffee (Tea on Request)
Milk and Crackers for Children

DINNER

Beef Broth with Barley
Roast Beef
Lima Beans-Potatoes
Bread and Butter
Milk and Crackers for Children

SUPPER

Hamburger Steak, Onion Sauce
Bread and Butter
Tea (Coffee or Milk)
Milk and crackers for Children

Milk and Crackers will be
served to
children between the regular
meals.

MONDAY, JULY 2, 1917

BREAKFAST

Apple Sauce
Oatmeal Served in Soup Plates
Bread and Butter
Coffee (Tea on Request)
Milk and Crackers for Children

DINNER

Rice Soup
Boiled Mutton with Brown Gravy
Green Peas-Potatoes
Bread and Butter
Milk and Crackers for Children

SUPPER

Pork and Beans, N.Y. Style
Stewed Fruit
Bread and Butter
Tea (Coffee on Request)
Milk and Crackers for Children

Milk and Crackers will be
served to
children between the regular
meals.

WEDNESDAY, SEPTEMBER 16, 1953

BREAKFAST

Stewed Pears
Rice Krispies
Fresh Milk
Dry Toast
Oleo
Assorted Bread and Coffee

DINNER

Cream of Spinach Soup
Vienna Meat Roast
Jardiniere Sauce
Harvard Beets
Boiled Potatoes
Ice Cream and Coffee

SUPPER

Barley Soup
Sardines in Oil
Tomato Sauce
Health Salad
Home Fried Potatoes
Assorted Bread
Cookies and Cocoa

Sadie Schultz in the kosher kitchen at Ellis Island.

The Seder At Ellis Island sponsored by the *Hebrew Immigrant Aid Society*, April 28, 1913.

From Genevieve Anderson of Levittown, New York:

I have hesitated in writing to you, as what I know about Ellis Island really concerns more about the people who worked there.

My father, Fred Hepting, worked at Ellis Island up until the time of his death in 1936. I spent many happy visits there, but the best was at Christmas. A fabulous concert was held for the immigrants in the big hall. Lucrezia Bori, Giovanni Martinelli, Madame Schuman-Heink have performed in various years. There was an orchestra on the stage and a beautifully decorated tree. After the concert, the immigrants received a gift of a drawstring bag containing small but useful items. The children received a bag also, plus a red mesh stocking filled with Christmas candy. Who arranged this, I'll never know.

I have yet to read that anyone ever appreciated the kind people who worked there and tried to make it easier for them. There was Mrs. Pratt, a teacher who held classes for the children to learn a few basic words in English. I was surprised to see how fast they could repeat and understand what she was doing. There was, also, an outdoor playground for them.

Even convicts being deported received, besides their meals, attention. I remember being surprised that the cell doors were open. I was in the company of Miss Brooks who supplied them with materials to help them pass the time. She even taught some to knit, not with needles, but a relic of today's lap knitting machine. I was fascinated and wholly delighted when one of them had my father give me a sweater vest that was knitted for me.

My father was not a government employee. He worked as a steward for the commissary contracted to a Mr. McGowan, (I spell it this way as I never saw it written) to feed immigrants. There was a kosher kitchen with a Mrs. Schultz in charge. She did the cooking and cleaning of dishes, pots, and tableware. Near this kitchen, tables were set for the religious Jewry. Every Passover for the nights of the seder, a rabbi officiated at the meal. Those nights my father did not come home as they ended quite late.

My father was a linguist. He spoke German, Polish, Russian, and could communicate in the various Slovak dialects, but was also fluent in Yiddish.

I don't know if this helps you material-wise - just remember these are the memories of a young child, now an elderly woman who is partially deaf. That's why this letter.

Dining Room at Ellis Island

Women and Children in the Dining Room at Ellis Island

The Foreign Language Sign in English, German, Italian, Polish, and Spanish.

ABOUT THE RECIPES

When we were trained as tour guides at Ellis Island, it was some time before the restoration began. The buildings had been vandalized; old equipment and furnishings had been scattered about. I distinctly remember being instructed that we were not to move any objects or disturb them in any way. This was to insure the accurate, historic restoration that was to follow. Though most items seemed little more than debris to the untrained eye, they could provide valuable clues as to a room's use and history to a restorer.

Years later, when I decided to compile this cookbook and sent out press releases announcing the recipe search, many newspapers wrote about the search and the recipes started to arrive.

As I read the recipes and stories that accompanied them, I quickly realized that these were more than "family favorites." Although I had originally planned on testing the recipes, it became apparent that these were historical documents and, as such, should be altered as little as possible. Any changes I made would be arbitrary and certainly of no use to future food historians. I did, however, want to standardize the recipes and make them more readable and usable to the public. Therefore, I have presented the recipes in standard cookbook format but with as few changes as possible.

The recipes that follow are only some of the many sent to me. I have tried to include various types of foods with stories of interest to the reader. All of the recipes I received, and any that I receive in the future, will be donated to the Ellis Island Museum and be made available to scholars and historians.

AUSTRIA
CZECHOSLOVAKIA
GERMANY
HUNGARY
LITHUANIA
POLAND
ROMANIA
RUSSIA
YUGOSLAVIA

From Sidney Hauser of New York, New York:

Thank you for your card concerning Ellis Island in general.

Did my relatives arrive at Ellis Island? No sir. But I did in year 1920.

Please permit me to mention that I was born May 17, 1900 in Austria.

Yes, I passed last year age 90 and my mind is as perfect as 50 years ago. I alone am typing my letter to you.

I left Europe July 22, 1920 on my way to America.

And when I came to Danzig there were no liners to leave for the U.S.A.

So I went with a American freighter with the name Susquehanna. After traveling close to 3 weeks on the ocean.

The ship arrived in New Yorker Port, September 19, 1920, one day before Yom Kippur.

I left the ship with many other immigrants, to Ellis Island.

A very huge room to be checked. As I stood in front of the judge.

He asked me to read a book in front of him, to be sure I can read. The judge never asked me how much money I have.

And neither did he ask me if I have a trade?

And the judge said to me you may leave and good luck to you young man.

I had only 2 dollars to my name.

And when I came outside, I saw the ocean in front of me.

I started to cry, my luck a representative from the HIAS took me with him.

And the HIAS kept me until over Yom Kippur.

The next day I visited relatives in Rivington street.

I sent home to my folks a telegram which cost me $1.90.

And all I had change was 10 cents to my name.

Soon I got a job as a busboy in a cafeteria.

My daily hours work was from 7 a.m. until 7 p.m.

My weekly pay was $16.00 and every two weeks a half day off.

And July 1921 brought my younger brother over, and he had to also to Ellis Island. But I had to pick him up to take him with me. And in 1923 I met a young girl her name was Vera Klein.

She too came from Austria. But she did not go to Ellis Island.

She came second class. And in 1926 I married Vera Klein.

Vera gave birth to two sons.

Vera passed away December 1961.

And today I have a beautiful family of children, grandchildren and great grandchildren. I retired December 1985.

I live alone all the years. I do not look my age and feeling great.

And I love America. Sir, I would love to visit you in your office. Sir, thank you for taking the time to read my letter.

And please forgive my typing mistakes.

God Bless You. Respectfully Yours,

Sidney Hauser

From Susan M. Dinkel of Sebewaing, Michigan:

Here is a recipe of my late mother, Mary Essler Bernhardt. She came from Austria via Ellis Island in 1908 at age twelve with her mother and other siblings to join her father, who had come to the U.S.A. earlier. They settled in Huron County, Michigan. They brought their expertise in struddle making from Austria and it is a great treat down through fourth and fifth generations.

STRUDDLE

6 cups all-purpose flour
2 cups lukewarm water
2 tsp. salt

2 tbsp. vegetable oil
1/4 cup melted butter

Put flour on board or in large bowl. Make well in center and pour combined water, oil and salt into well - mix with fork and make soft dough, add more flour if necessary. Knead on floured board until smooth and elastic. Divide into 4 parts, knead into smooth balls. Roll each to about 1/2" thick oval. Brush each piece with melted lard. Cover with waxed paper and let stand in warm place while preparing fillings.

Then put 1 oval piece on lightly floured table cloth (on table) and stretch dough gradually from center while walking around the table. Snip off thick edges, when dough is stretched thin as paper.

Sprinkle with filling, drizzle with 1/4 cup melted butter. Fold about 1" of dough on long side then pick up the edge of table cloth on that side and the dough can be rolled - like a jelly roll. Put in well-greased cake pan or cookie sheet and bake at 375° about 1/2 hour or until lightly browned and filling is done. Enough for 4.

Apple Filling

1 quart cooking apples,
 peeled and cut fine
1/2 cup sugar

Combine and sprinkle
 on stretched dough.

Cheese Filling (Enough for 2)

2 lbs. cottage cheese
3/4 cup sugar
4 eggs

Mix and drizzle
 over stretched dough.

From Anna Knarr of Floral Park, New York:

This recipe has been passed down for many generations. It is quite simple, and I make them very often.

AUSTRIAN NUSS-KIPFERL (NUT CRESCENT COOKIES)

3 1/2 cups all-purpose flour
1 1/2 cups confectioners' sugar
3 sticks sweet (unsalted) butter (3/4 lb.)
3 egg yolks
5 oz. ground walnuts
1 tsp. vanilla extract

Place all ingredients in a large mixing bowl and knead by hand until well blended. Place a piece of the dough on a cookie board and roll by hand into a log approximately 1 1/2" to 2" in diameter. Cut the log into even slices using a knife. Roll each slice, using the palm of your hand, into finger-thick mini logs on the cookie board and shape like a crescent. Grease your cookie sheet. Evenly space the cookies, but not too close. Bake at 350° until golden at the edges.

Optional -- before serving, roll each cookie in regular granulated sugar.

From Marie Gardiner of Leonardtown, Maryland:

The Ruzicka Family came from Austria-Hungary to Philadelphia, Pennsylvania, in 1907.

My grandmother, Mary Theresa Fazekas-Ruzicka, was an excellent cook and prepared all of the family meals. Her daughters practiced on their own only while raising their own families.

My mother, Blanche Marie Ruzicka-Rigling, was more democratic. She let us all help in the kitchen, which helped each of us three children become adept at meal selection, preparation, and nutrition. I became a Home Economist, a result of this early exposure.

The following is a cookie and a fruitcake recipe the family gave as gifts at Christmastime for many years. We started at the end of October and continued production of cookies until the middle of December. My mother was responsible for everyone doing their part correctly, while our father donned heavy cotton gloves, taking the trays from the oven and replacing them with unbaked cookie-filled trays. He slid the cookies off with a thin-bladed knife, and my brother, being the youngest, placed the cookies on clean, brown paper bags until cooled, and then in tins for storage. My sister used the cookie press to form all kinds of shapes from colored dough provided her, while I decorated the tops, cut up candied fruit for the cake, and ground nuts. When we get together now and nibble on cookies, we laugh and say, "This is a broken one" or "This is a burnt one," because that was what we could eat our fill of during this mass-production time. We have fond thoughts of those years when both parents worked to educate us, and each of us children played several instruments, sang, and were active in school athletics and other activities.

SPRITZ COOKIES

4 cups sifted cake flour
1 tsp. baking powder
3/4 cup butter
3/4 cup shortening

1 cup sugar
1 egg, beaten
2 tsp. vanilla extract

Sift together flour and baking powder; cream butter, shortening and sugar until very light. Add egg and vanilla; mix thoroughly. Stir in dry ingredients; mix thoroughly. Put dough through a pastry tube or cookie press onto ungreased cookie sheets. If desired, decorate with colored sugar, candied fruit, etc. Bake in hot oven (400°) about 10 minutes or until lightly browned. Makes about 6 dozen.

FRUITCAKE

2 cups sifted cake flour
1 tsp. baking powder
1 tsp. baking soda
1 cup brown sugar
1 1/4 cups water
1 cup seeded raisins
1/2 cup candied peel, finely cut

1/3 cup shortening
1 tsp. ground cinnamon
1/2 tsp. ground cloves
1/2 tsp. grated nutmeg
1/2 tsp. salt
1/2 cup chopped nuts (optional)

Sift together flour, baking powder and baking soda. Combine sugar, water, raisins, peel, shortening, cinnamon, cloves, nutmeg, salt, and nuts. Boil for 3 minutes; cool. Add dry ingredients; mix well. Put in well-greased tube pan about 9" in diameter; bake in slow oven (325°) about 55 minutes. Makes one 9" tube cake.

From Mary Alice Klein of Beaver, Pennsylvania:

I came to United States at age four through Ellis Island. I had to stay in the hospital alone. My mother went on ahead. I got the childhood disease. I came from Austria-Hungary, and this recipe came from my grandmother and has been handed down to my grandchildren. I serve this when unexpected company comes. It is quick!

PALACHINKAS

2 cups milk
2 cups all-purpose flour
2 eggs, beaten
2 tbsp. sugar

1 tsp. salt
1 tsp. vanilla
shortening

Thin batter, small skillet. Melt 1/2 tbsp. shortening in skillet. Pour batter, about 1/4 cup at a time. Fry on both sides. Spread favorite jelly and roll.

From Audrey Eisdorfer of Hallandale, Florida:

My grandmother was born in Austria in the year 1900. Grandma Lillie came to America as a young girl in 1914. She made knubble (garlic) borscht from scratch using fresh beets, but she adapted this easy recipe in her later years. She passed away recently, but her memory will always remain with us especially when we enjoy her special soup. She was very proud of her Jewish heritage!

GRANDMA LILLIE'S EASY KNUBBLE BORSCHT

2 quart jars of borscht with beets
2 8 oz. cans of beets, julienne or sliced
4 pieces of flanken with bones, cut into thirds
8 cloves of fresh garlic, minced
water

Into a soup pot, pour borscht. Add garlic, beets, and flanken. Add water to cover (approx. 2 cups). Bring to boil uncovered. Then cover and simmer for about 2 1/2 hours or till meat is tender. Serves 6-8. May be frozen.

From Hermine Sostarich of Brookfield, Wisconsin:

My mother, Barbara Suveljak Hosni, and father, Thomas Frank Hosni, Sr., passed through Ellis Island in September 1913 from Austria-Hungary. My mother decided I should have some of her recipes. As a result, we did a "stop and measure" as she prepared Nut Roll.

CROATIAN NUT ROLL (ORAHNJACA)

6 cups unbleached flour
1/2 tsp. salt
1/2 cup sugar
1 cup light cream
3/4 cup water
4 egg yolks, beaten
2 oz. cake yeast
1/2 cup water
1/4 lb. unsalted butter, melted
1 1/2 tbsp. sugar
1 tbsp. sour cream
1 egg yolk

Filling
1 lb. walnuts, finely ground
1 cup sugar
1/2 stick butter, melted
1/2 to 1 cup milk
2 egg whites, beaten
1/4 tsp. walnut flavoring

Sift together flour, salt and 1/2 cup sugar in a large mixing bowl. Heat cream and 3/4 cup water until lukewarm. Add egg yolks and melted butter. Dissolve yeast in 1/2 cup lukewarm water, and 1 1/2 tbsp. sugar and add the egg mixture. Make a well into the flour, slowly pour yeast mixture into the flour beating well with wooden spoon. On a slightly floured board knead dough until it is elastic and smooth. If dough sticks to the board, add a little flour, knead 15 to 20 minutes. Place dough in a large bowl lightly greased, turning to grease top. Cover with a towel and let rise until double in bulk. Punch dough down. On a slightly floured board shape into a ball, then divide ball in half. Now shape each piece into a smooth ball. Place 1 ball in bowl and cover with a towel. Place the other on a slightly floured board, cover and let rest 5 to 10 minutes. Now roll as for jelly roll 11" x 5", spread the nut filling (after mixing ingredients well) and start rolling, rolling away from and pulling roll towards you each time you make a turn. Place in a greased pan 11" x 5", seam side down, prick about 10 times with a fork to release air. Brush with 1 egg yolk mixed with 1 tbsp. of sour cream. Cover and let rise until double in bulk. Bake at 350° for 45 minutes to 1 hour. Other ball can be filled with other filling.

From Mary Ann Knight of West Aliquippa, Pennsylvania:

My mom and grandparents came from a small town in Czechoslovakia in 1911. Ever since that sea voyage, Mom doesn't want to take a boat ride or go near water.

Down through the years we've enjoyed hearing my grandfather's stories. He, as well as Mom, spoke Slovak often at our home. Many delicious recipes were served during our years together, as well as special holiday meals.

It truly is a rich experience having ethnic heritage passed down to myself and I'll try to keep passing traditions down to my son and his family.

This recipe is just one of the many, inexpensive eating enjoyments we used for years. These pioneers deserve any recognition possible. All eyes are on Europe again.

GRANDMA'S GREENBEAN SOUP

2 cups fresh garden green beans or
 1 large can green beans (if can used, drain beans)
4 white potatoes, diced and peeled
1 quart less 1/2 cup milk
1/2 medium onion, diced

Cook potatoes and beans till tender. Drain beans and potatoes. Add the milk. Mix 1/2 cup milk with 5 tablespoons of flour to make a gravy of white sauce consistency. To this sauce, add the butter and the onions. Brown this, then add the beans, potatoes, and rest of milk. Let simmer for 10 minutes. Then serve. Makes at least 10 servings.

Smells wonderful, tastes delicious.

From Gladys E. Kocs of West Allis, Wisconsin:

AUNT BETTY'S (HRUBY) KOLACKY DOUGH

Bulk Bakers Yeast, 7 cent size -- use better than half, or two envelopes (1/4 oz. each) active dry yeast
1 tsp. sugar
1 cup lukewarm water

Mix the above.

Then scald 1 cup milk
6 tbsp. shortening
1/3 cup sugar

1 level tbsp. salt
7 cups all-purpose flour
3 eggs, well beaten

Dissolve yeast in lukewarm water and 1 tsp. sugar. Scald milk, add shortening, sugar and salt. Stir well and add 2 cups flour. Beat well until smooth. Add yeast and well-beaten eggs. Beat well again. Add remaining flour (to make a soft dough). Let rise and make kolacky or cinnamon roll or clover leaf rolls.

AUNT BETTY'S PRUNE FILLING

2 lbs. prunes (cook and put through food chopper)
add 1 cup applesauce
3/4 cup sugar
1/2 tsp. cinnamon and chopped nuts

AUNT BETTY'S COTTAGE CHEESE FILLING

1 lb. dry cottage cheese
2 egg yolks, beaten
1 egg, beaten
6 tbsp. sugar

dash salt
pinch each nutmeg & cinnamon
white raisins (optional)

Mix and fill kolacky. Bake at 375° for 25 minutes or until browned. Brush with melted buter.

From Mrs. Helen P. Koza of Depew, New York:

Here is a recipe brought from Czechoslovakia by my mother, Mary Thnat Pavlochik. She arrived July 12, 1920, on the Lafayette.

My mother knew this recipe for Nut Horns by heart. I had to watch and translate. They are delicious and we all loved them.

KIFLES (NUT ROLLS OR HORNS)

4 cups all-purpose flour
2 cakes yeast, or two envelopes (1/4 oz. each) active dry yeast
1 cup butter
4 egg yolks (save whites)
1 cup sour cream
1 cup powdered sugar
1/2 cup granulated sugar

Filling

2 cups ground nuts
1 cup sugar
4 egg whites, stiffly beaten
1 tsp. vanilla

Combine nuts, sugar & vanilla. Fold in the stiffly beaten egg whites. Set aside till ready to make the kifles. Put sifted flour into large bowl. Crumble the yeast into the egg yolks (in small container) and let the yeast soften. Cut butter into the flour till crumbly. Add egg yolks & yeast & sour cream. Mix well until it forms a smooth ball. Form into 10 balls & chill. Mix 1 cup powdered sugar & 1/2 cup granulated sugar. On board or tabletop sprinkle a spoonful of sugar mixture, place 1 ball on the sugar, add more sugar on top, then roll ball out. Roll until dough is 1/8 " thick, forming a circle. Cut the circle into 8 pie-shaped wedges. Fill wide end of each wedge with 1 level teaspoon of filling -- then roll up from wide end to point. Continue with all the balls. Place on greased sheets. Bake at 325° for 15 minutes.

From Anna L. Langsather of Roundup, Montana:

This is a recipe that my mother brought from Czechoslovakia to America through Ellis Island in 1904. When she landed, she kissed the ground, so happy to be here in a free country. She was an excellent cook.

PIROKY

1 cup all-purpose flour
1 egg
1/4 tsp. salt
4 tbsp. cold water (approx.)

Mix all ingredients with enough water to make a medium soft dough. Knead well, then roll out until thin. Cut in squares to make 50 piroky. Place on each square 1 teaspoon of filling, fold in half to make triangles. Pinch edges well to keep filling from escaping. Drop in boiling water and cook until piroky rise to the top of water, then cook 5 minutes longer. When done pour a small amount of cold water and strain in colander. Brown melted butter and pour over piroky when served.

Cheese filling

1/2 cup dry cottage cheese
1 egg yolk
1 tsp. butter
pinch of salt

Combine ingredients and mix well.

Cabbage filling

1 lb. cabbage, chopped fine
1/2 tsp. salt
1 tbsp. butter
1 tsp. sugar

Add salt to cabbage, set aside to stand for 15 minutes. Then squeeze out water from cabbage and fry in butter that has browned. Add sugar and stir occasionally to keep from burning. Fry until golden brown.

From Ingrid Jacoba Smith of Port St. Lucie, Florida:

My German great-grandmother was by all accounts a wonderful cook. My mother has several of her recipes, but my all-time favorites were her Christmas cookies. Her name was Ida Werner nee Goldschmidt, and she came to Buffalo, New York, as an unmarried young girl of seventeen in 1889 from Hanover.

LITTLE GRANDMA'S ANISSCHNITTE

4 egg whites
1 cup sugar
1/2 lemon (rind and juice)
2 tsp. anise seed

6 egg yolks
2 cups all-purpose flour
1/2 tsp. baking powder

Beat egg whites stiff, slowly add sugar, then yolks, keep beating and add juice and grated rind. Then add flour, anise seed, and baking powder. Grease and flour a 16" x 10" pan. Spread dough evenly and bake 15-20 minutes at 350°. Cut into bars and toast in oven at 350° until slightly golden.

From Anna E. Fontana of Matamoras, Pennsylvania:

My grandmother came over from northern Germany and she baked this delicious cake.

HESSEN CRUMB CAKE

2 cups all-purpose flour
1 cup sugar
1 tbsp. cloves
1/2 tsp. nutmeg
1/2 cup butter

1 egg
2 tbsp. molasses
1 cup sour milk
1 tsp. baking soda

Mix flour, sugar, spices and butter together with a fork or (as my grandmother did) with your hands, until blended. Reserve half of mixture for top of cake. To other half, add well-beaten egg, molasses, and sour milk to which the baking soda has been added. Mix well and pour into greased 8" x 8" pan. Dough will be thin and easy to pour. Sprinkle reserve mixture on top. Bake 35 minutes at 350°.

From Myrtle E. Cavallo of Danbury, Connecticut:

My father, Robert Totz, had just turned sixteen when he left Germany to come to America, about 1905. He was in steerage but met a young benefactress traveling first class. When she realized he did not have the required $25.00 to enter the country, she gave him the money but wanted to marry him.

I asked, "Why didn't you?" He replied, "She was too old." I said, "How old was she?" "Nineteen!"

KNOCKWURST & NOODLES

1 lb. cooked knockwurst, cut in strips
1 onion
1 tsp. horseradish (or more, to taste)
salt & pepper, to taste
1 can tomato soup
3/4 cup water
1/4 lb. cheddar cheese
1/2 lb. cooked noodles

Chop and fry onion in butter. Mix together all ingredients except noodles and cook over low flame until cheese melts. Add cooked noodles and serve. Serves 8.

From Floramae Burke Elliff of Glen Carbon, Illinois:

My maternal grandmother came from Colmar, Alsace-Lorraine. She was born a Frenchwoman, but after the Franco-Prussian War, she was raised as a German. She came to America about 1893 or early 1894. We only know that she went through Ellis Island and then on to New Jersey. Her beau had come to America before her and they both worked on a farm...she hated that! Sometime between her arrival in America and the birth of my mother, Albertina Maurer Burke, the couple moved to the St. Louis area. My mother was born in East Saint Louis, Illinois, February 23, 1895. The family continued to live in this area, moving from time to time and the few of us who are still living are in the same county. We have done a bit of research on my grandmother but cannot place her in any exact time of arrival, nor name of the ship. This is too bad as we now have grandchildren who are interested in genealogy...hoping they are able to carry this farther than we were able to do.

My grandmother, Caroline Lux Maurer, never cooked from a recipe but when I married I urged her so strongly to tell me 'how to make' some of her recipes that she gave me a by-guess-and-by-golly recipe for several things, among them a particular favorite of mine, Rolled Steak.

ROLLED STEAK

2 lbs. round steak
6 bay leaves
onions

Two pounds round steak, pounded until thin and shaped into a large disk or "round". On this ring of meat place 2 large onions, cut into slices about 1/4 inch thick and separated into rings. Over this place 6 bay leaves for flavoring. Roll meat around onions and bay leaves as for a jelly roll. Tie with string, and brown in small amount of hot fat in a large cast-iron dutch oven. When browned on all sides, turn heat down, add about 1 cup water, cover tightly and simmer until meat is tender...about 1 hour. Remove meat from pot and keep warm on warmed platter.

If necessary add more water to pot...not too much as it will weaken the gravy. With roux of flour and water, thicken gravy, darken with graviaid if desired and pour a small amount over the rolled meat. Serve remaining gravy as side dish with hot home made noodles...or mashed potatoes.

From Christine Kindel of Greendale, Wisconsin:

I came through Ellis Island in May 27, 1927, from Austria. I was a scared girl of seventeen years going to Milwaukee, Wisconsin, to meet my relatives. Today I still live in Wisconsin.

ROTKRAUT (SWEET AND SOUR RED CABBAGE)

1 head red cabbage (2 lbs.), shredded
2 tbsp. bacon drippings
1 small onion, chopped fine
1/2 cup wine vinegar
3 medium-size apples, peeled and cubed
1/2 cup brown sugar
2 tbsp. corn starch
1 1/2 cups water

Shred cabbage, put in colander, and pour 2 quarts boiling water over it, drain. In large skillet, put in the bacon drippings, add the onion, and fry till transparent. Add cabbage. Add the rest of the ingredients and simmer for 30 minutes. Mix 2 tbsp. corn starch with 1 1/2 cups water and add to the red cabbage. Simmer for 5 minutes longer. Serves 4-6 people.

From Gloria D. Felton of Lincoln, Illinois:

My father was born in Zetel, Germany, September 18, 1907. His name was Friedrich Arnold Weidhuner and he came here in October of 1924 on the S.S. President Harding at the age of seventeen from Bremerhaven by way of Ellis Island. He shortened his first name to Fred for the American way.

Dad had a sister and a brother-in-law that left Hamburg, Germany, about the same time he left, and they were lucky enough they all met at Ellis Island. Another sister and brother came in 1923. All of those named above settled in central Illinois.

My dad was able to go to Germany in 1967 and 1977 for a visit as he has two brothers and lots of other relatives still living there. My dad's father came for a visit in 1955. When he returned to Germany he told the family he had been through "Heaven and Hell" as he had made the trip by plane and my dad had taken him on a tour of the coal mine where he worked. Opa (Grandfather) also told the family people were backward in the U.S.A. because "they eat outside and go in the house to the bathroom."

This recipe was one of my dad's favorites.

GERMAN CREAMED PEAS

1 can peas
milk
1 tbsp. corn starch

1 tbsp. butter
1 tsp. minced onion
5 slices crisp fried bacon, crumbled

Drain peas saving 1/4 cup of liquid, adding milk sufficient to cover peas in pan. Stir in corn starch while peas are cold. Heat on low while stirring till mixture thickens. Add butter, onions, bacon, and black pepper (if desired). Simmer on low heat, stirring often, for 3-4 minutes.

From Dolores Peterson of Cedar Rapids, Iowa:

OPEN FACE BAVARIAN PEACH PIE

4 cups fresh, canned or frozen peaches
 (peeled, sliced and arranged in baked pie shell)
1/4 cup minute tapioca or cornstarch
1 tsp. cinnamon
1/2 cup sugar
dash salt
1 cup heavy cream

Mix tapioca, cinnamon, sugar, and salt. Add cream. Let set for 5 minutes.
Cook over low heat stirring. Bring just to boil. Pour over peaches. Bake at
350°, 35 to 45 minutes. Test for doneness. Place foil rim around crust if it
becomes too brown.

S.S. PRESIDENT HARDING

From Mrs. Ronald W. Goretzke of Elizabethtown, Pennsylvania:

John Goretzke, born 1874 in Germany, came to America through Ellis Island. He walked the Pennsylvania Rail Road to Altoona and worked in the coal mines. While passing Lancaster County in Pennsylvania on route to Altoona, he saw the desirable farm land, so when his debt was paid for his passage, he walked back to Lancaster County and hired himself out to an Amish farmer. He remained here the remainder of his life. He later married Katie Eichlerberger, whose parents also came from Germany and arrived at Ellis Island.

BUTTONS

2 cups all-purpose flour
1 tbsp. salt
1 egg, beaten

Make it into a paste with milk. Keep on dry side. Drop on boiling sauerkraut.

PICKLED BEETS

Cook red beets (with skins on) till soft. Save the water in which they were cooked. Strain it and add it to the red beets after they are peeled. Put enough red beets for about 2 quarts in a large kettle and add:

1 cup sugar   3/4 cup vinegar
3/4 tsp. salt   1/4 tsp. pepper

Put beets in jars, cover with strained juice. Bring to a full boil before pouring over beets in the jar. Seal.

HOT MILK SPONGE CAKE

2 cups sugar
4 eggs
2 cups all-purpose flour
3 tsp. baking powder

1/2 tsp. salt
1 cup milk, scalded
2 tbsp. butter
1 tsp. vanilla

Beat eggs till light and fluffy. Add sugar and beat again. Add flour, salt, and baking powder, which have been sifted together. Add scalded milk, add butter and vanilla. Put in greased and floured loaf pan. Bake 350° for 45 minutes.

MOLASSES CRUMB PIE (SHOOFLY PIE)

1 cup molasses
1 cup hot water
1 tsp. baking soda, dissolved in hot water

Crumbs

3 cups all-purpose flour
1 1/2 cups brown sugar
1 tsp. cinnamon
shortening, size of an egg

Mix half of crumbs with liquid. Remaining crumbs go on top. Bake at 375° for 45 minutes. Makes two 9" pies.

From Shirley A. Kopp of Glen Ellyn, Illinois:

My grandmother, Anna Raum Stegmayer, was born on April 5, 1879, near Thueringen, Germany. In 1894, she came to the U.S. through Ellis Island and then settled in Chicago. My mother, Charlotte, was so very much like my grandmother, Anna. Both my granny and my mom were wonderful mothers, housekeepers, cooks, and bakers. I do believe their philosophy was "Love is not love until you give it away."

These recipes originally came from my great-grandmother Raum of Thueringen, Germany. In turn, they were given to my grandmother. Then, she gave them to my mother, Charlotte Emma Stegmayer Jacobs, of America. In turn, she gave them to me and I've passed them on to Anna's great-grandchildren here in America.

GERMAN EGG PANCAKES

3 large eggs
3/4 cup milk
3/4 cup all-purpose flour

1/4 tsp. baking powder
1/3 tsp. salt
1 tbsp. melted butter

Beat eggs, beat milk in, and then beat flour in gradually. Add baking powder, salt and butter. Put a little bacon grease in pan each time. Take 4 or 5 tablespoons of batter, tip and roll pan. Fry on 1 side, then flip over. Spread either grape or other jelly on or you can also spread sugar or syrup. Lingonberries are good, too. Makes approximately 6.

POTATO PANCAKES

3 large potatoes
1 large onion (sweet preferred)

Grate above ingredients. Skim off water.

Add:

1/2 tsp. salt
1 egg
1 tbsp. all-purpose flour

Mix salt, egg and flour. Mix with potatoes and onions. Fry in a little bacon grease each time. Serve with applesauce and bacon or whatever you wish.

GERMAN POTATO SALAD

5 or 6 medium potatoes, boiled & peeled
 (white or red - not Idaho)
1/2 lb. bacon, cut into small pieces
1 tbsp. all-purpose flour
3/4 cup vinegar
1/4 cup water
1/4 - 1/2 cup sugar, to taste
salt & pepper, to taste
3 or 4 green onions, sliced, with stems
 or 1 small sweet onion, chopped

Boil potatoes with jackets on, drain, cool slightly and then peel and slice. While potatoes are boiling, make sauce as follows: cut up bacon in small pieces and fry out until almost crisp. Drain off most of grease. Add flour, tanning slightly. Add vinegar, water, sugar, salt and pepper. After this is all mixed, add onion. Keep cooking and stirring until sauce is thickened (taste to your preference). Pour hot mixture over sliced, boiled potatoes. Can garnish above with hard boiled eggs and then, if preferred, sprinkle a little paprika on sliced eggs. By making and experimenting a couple of times, you'll find just exactly how you most prefer seasonings. Be sure there's plenty of sauce. Serves approximately 4.

SOUR MILK DOUGHNUTS

1 heaping tbsp. butter, melted
1 cup sugar
2 eggs
1 cup sour milk*
1 level tsp. baking soda in milk
1 heaping tsp. baking powder
dash of freshly grated nutmeg
3 1/2 cups (approx.) flour (to stiffen enough to handle)

Roll out dough and use doughnut cutter. Fry in 1 lb. of fresh boiling lard. Use one of holes to test boiling lard. After doughnuts are slightly cool, sprinkle with powdered sugar, if desired.

* Use lemon juice or vinegar to sour the milk.

From Willis and Joanne Krieger of Portland, Oregon:

This recipe is a family favorite that was used when our German ancestors lived in Russia more than 200 years ago. We use it as a main dish complemented by fruit or fruit salad. It's a hearty meal filled with memories of those dear people who worked so hard, tilling the soil to grow the cabbage and onions, tending, thrashing, and grinding the wheat, butchering the pigs for lard and the cows for hamburger, gathering the eggs, and carrying the water from the stream or well. How easy we have it today!

KRAUT KUCHEN

2 cups milk, scalded
1 cup shortening
1/2 cup sugar
3 tsp. salt
1 cup water
4 cups all-purpose flour

2 large eggs
2 pkgs. active dry yeast (1/4 oz. each)
1 tsp. sugar
4 1/2 - 5 cups all-purpose flour

In large bowl, pour milk over shortening to melt. Add next 4 ingredients.

Beat with electric beater until well blended. Add 2 large eggs (room temperature), 2 pkgs. yeast dissolved in 1 cup warm water and 1 tsp. sugar. Gradually add 4 1/2 to 5 cups of flour. Use the mixer until too stiff to turn. Then continue kneading the dough until all flour is used. Grease bowl and turn dough. Cover and let rise until double in bulk. Punch down, let rise, do this twice. Let rise a third time, then divide dough in half and roll each on large floured board. Cut into squares. Fill centers with 1/2 cup filling. Pinch together tightly. Place each on well-greased pan. Let rise, bake 30 minutes in 375° oven.

Filling

2 medium heads of cabbage, chopped
2 large onions, browned lightly, seasoned with salt & pepper
2 lbs. ground round, lightly browned
2 tsp. salt
1\2 tsp. pepper

From Frieda Mair of Ocala, Florida:

I arrived on October 20, 1929. I spent one night on Ellis Island and went from there to Chicago. I never forgot that night on Ellis Island. I never regretted that I came to this country.

GERMAN APPLE CAKE

1 3/4 cups all-purpose flour
2 tsp. baking powder
1/2 tsp. salt
3/4 cup sugar

1 1/2 sticks butter
2 eggs
6 apples, sliced

Mix that well and lay out a form 8" x 12". Slice apples and cover the form with apples.

2 eggs, separated
1/2 cup sugar

1 tsp. vanilla
1/2 cup sour cream

Beat 2 egg yolks with a 1/2 cup sugar, 1 tsp. vanilla. Beat the egg whites separately. Fold in 1/2 cup sour cream and then the egg white. Spread that over the apples. Bake at 400°, 25 to 30 minutes until golden brown.

From Anne Roesch Larson of Aberdeen, South Dakota:

My parents were Frederick and Rosina Treftz from Russia who came through Ellis Island in 1898. Their parents were born in Germany.

This I remember so clearly as they told it to us. They came from Glucksdahl, Russia. Were both born there. My father became an orphan at the age of seven. He told us how hungry he was at times. He would go from house to house and pick up the crumbs of bread the women swept out their door sill, he would eat these crumbs. To this day, I cannot put any crumbs or bread into the garbage. Throw it to the birds. They had three children: John, age six, Frederick, age three, and Rose, age two. Three days before they sailed, little Frederick died of a brain tumor. His name was on the passport. My parents never spoke of his death without weeping; they did not cry, they wept. They came to Ellis Island on the ship "Keiser Wilhelm," sailing from Bremen on September 26, 1898. They were on the ocean for twenty-eight days. I do not know the date they arrived at Ellis Island, but their boy, John, had an eye infection and Mother and John and Rose were held over at the island until John's eyes were healed . Father was sent on to New York with the rest of the people from the ship. Imagine what Mother went through all alone with two infants at the island. Mother and the children met Father in New York. On October 26, 1898, they arrived at Hillsview, South Dakota, where they were met by Henry Gross, brother-in-law of Frederick Roesch. They came by train to Hillsview, South Dakota. After Hillsview, they moved to a farm with some friends, seven miles east of Eureka. On April 22, 1899, they moved to a farm five miles north of Roscoe, which was a cattle ranch.

They lived there until the death of my father on November 25, 1930. Mother continued to live there with her youngest son until 1944, when she came to Aberdeen to live with me. Father was thirty years old when he came to the United States, Mother twenty-eight. He died at age sixty-two, she at age eighty-five. They had fourteen children. Three died in Russia, two in South Dakota. Nine of us grew up on this farm. John and Rose were born in Russia. I was the only one that was delivered by a doctor. We all were given an education to make our living. Our father insisted on this. When my brother John returned from Germany after WWI, he recalled having seen the Statue Of Liberty before as a child. During WWI we were called Russians by some people in the little town of Roscoe. My father went to the Bank and asked how many Liberty Bonds the Judge had bought and then bought twice as many as the Judge had bought. After that the people were kinder. Germans-from-Russia have contributed their very best to this area. I'm very proud of my heritage.

GOOD FRIDAY SUPPER

Homemade noodles cooked in milk. Served with cooked, dried prunes.

Our flour was ground from our own wheat. My father would leave the farm in a large double-box wagon or sled and drive to a flour mill twenty-five miles away and came home late at night with large 100-lb. sacks of flour ground from the wheat he had taken over. He did this in the fall of the year so that there would be enough flour for all winter for this family of nine children, my parents, and many people who would be traveling through.

Noodles

Beat 3 eggs, add 3 tbsp. milk and 1 tsp. salt. With a spoon, stir in as much flour as possible, then turn on board and knead in as much flour to make a stiff dough. Roll very thin, into round sheets. Dry these on towels until dry, but flexible to roll into a roll like you would a jelly roll. With a sharp knife, cut roll into thin slices. Fluff and separate the noodles. Pour 2 quarts milk into large kettle, bring milk to boiling point, add the noodles and simmer until noodles are cooked, about 20 minutes. Serves 6-8.

Sometimes Mother cooked the noodles in water, drained them into a large bowl, added the cooked prunes, or raisins and covered them with fresh bread cubes browned in melted butter.

WINE SOUP

We were never allowed to have any wine as we were growing up except when we were sick. Mother made this wine soup for us, made with wine my parents made from grapes they had bought. In Russia, they raised their own grapes.

1 cup water
1 cup sweet red wine
a little sugar, if desired
1 egg
1/2 cup sweet cream

Beat one egg and add 1/2 cup sweet cream. Mix this with the water and wine, simmer a bit and serve over slices of toast.

STIRRUM

A one-dish meal served with fresh garden lettuce.

3 eggs, beaten
1 tbsp. sugar
1/2 tsp. salt
1/2 cup milk
1/2 tsp. baking powder
1 cup all-purpose flour

Mix all ingredients thoroughly. Pour all the batter into a black, iron skillet, which is heated over a low flame, with some melted shortening or oil to cover bottom of skillet. Fry the mixture but keep stirring it and breaking it into little pieces, until mixture is no longer sticky (moist) but crisp. Put into a large serving bowl.

Lettuce

Wash and dry chopped lettuce leaves. Put into large bowl, cover with dressing of 3/4 cup sour cream, dash of salt and 1 tbsp. vinegar. Add some sliced green onions. Stir and serve.

SCHLITZ KUECHLA

3/4 cup sugar
1/2 tsp. salt
3 tsp. baking powder
1 cup milk or cream
3 eggs
5 cups all-purpose flour

Mix and roll out on floured board. Cut into squares; in each square make 2 cuts in the center, not way out to the edge. Pull the ends through or twist. Deep fry in hot lard or other shortening, same as doughnuts. Sprinkle with sugar if desired. Makes about 2 dozen.

When Mother made these, it was our complete meal, served with cooked dried prunes or rice pudding.

From Janice Quivey of Portland, Oregon:

As I attempted to collect Grandmother's recipes, I was reminded that good cooks don't write down anything to pass on to the next generation! My mother recalls that the family food was plain, using the meats available and fruits and vegetables grown in their own gardens. To a special recipe she would have added "a handful of this and that with sprinkles of spices and salt." But she brought with her from Germany a fondness for apple pastries and cakes and all sorts of sweets which I surely inherited! I am sending two recipes that the family remembers smelling in their kitchens growing up. My grandmama, Sophie Schoonover, nee Brobiel, made this often. She called it "Golden Rod."

GOLDEN ROD

She cooked rice and made a white sauce. Hard boil eggs, chop the whites, put into the white sauce. Chop up the yolks and set aside. She poured the white sauce mixture over the hot rice and sprinkled the yolks over and served hot.

WALNUT CAKE

1/3 cup shortening
1 cup granulated sugar
2 cups sifted cake flour
1/2 tsp. baking powder
1/2 tsp. salt

1 tsp. vanilla
1/2 cup milk
1/2 cup chopped walnuts
3 egg whites

Cream together shortening and sugar. Sift flour and baking powder. Mix together salt, vanilla, and milk. Fold in walnuts and egg whites. Bake in loaf pan 45 minutes at 350° or in a 9" cake pan for 25 minutes at 350°. Dust with powdered sugar.

From Hans Semder of Valley Stream, New York:

My brother Heinz, age six, and I, age nine, arrived with our mother at Ellis Island in 1931. It was a stormy ten-day voyage from Germany, and we all jumped with joy at the sight of the Statue of Liberty. 1931 was a depression year, and as immigrants, we had to struggle to survive. That meant meat only on Sundays and soups the remaining six days. My mother had been a hotel cook in Germany, and the soups were meals in themselves and sufficiently nourishing. Now, fifty years later, my mother's outstanding and unusual string bean soup is still the favorite of our children and grandchildren.

MRS. SEMDER'S VERY OWN GERMAN STRING BEAN SOUP (A COMPLETE MEAL)

1/2 lb. bones
2 3/4 cups water
1 lb. beef (neck, shin, tail)
2 lbs. stringbeans
4 medium potatoes
salt, to taste

1 onion
1 leek
2 small carrots
1 piece celery
oregano, hearty pinch

Wash the bones, cover with the cold water and bring quickly to a boil. Turn down the heat and simmer for 1 hour. Put in the meat and a little salt, bring to a boil again, turn down heat and simmer for 1 1/2 - 2 hours. Clean carrot, celery, leek and onion (leave whole). Add to stock last hour of cooking. When the broth is done, strain through a fine sieve.

Cut meat into bite-size pieces. Add to broth. Add stringbeans that have been cleaned and cut into 1 " pieces. Add potatoes that have been peeled, and cut into quarters. Add a pinch of oregano. Simmer till potatoes and stringbeans are tender. Salt to taste.

From Ruth K. Schairer of Baldwinsville, New York:

Sometime on or about October 23, 1923, my mother arrived through Ellis Island and went on to Syracuse, New York. She was twenty-two years old at the time and was married to my father November 4, 1923. They had been engaged in Germany and had known each another since their early teen years.

One day, I asked Mother to write her recipe for "Spitz Bubben" (Rascals, in English). The enclosed is exactly as she wrote the recipe except to mention that raspberry jam was spread over the dough and strips of extra dough were interlaced over the top.

SPITZ BUBBEN (RASCALS)

3 cups all-purpose flour
2 tsp. baking powder
1 cup sugar
3/4 cup shortening
lemon rind
2 eggs

375° for 12-15 minutes.

From Carol M. Schacht of Petersburg, Illinois:

My grandparents arrived in New York in the 1920's from Germany. They came from near Breslow, Germany (now in Poland).

My grandfather was a blacksmith. He was painted by a famous American painter, Ivan Albright, originally from Illinois. The Carnegie Institute in Pittsburgh, Pennsylvania, has the painting. It's called "Among Those Left".

My grandmother said when she arrived at Ellis Island she had two boys holding on to her skirt on the right and two boys holding on the left (my dad and three uncles). She was carrying my aunt, then a baby, who had a cold at the time, so she was detained two weeks at Ellis Island.

Here are some favorite memories: sitting on my grandfather's lap in a chair, looking out the window while he ate and gave me bites of his oatmeal and rye bread, and picking potato bugs off plants with my grandfather. We would fill up buckets of these orange colored bugs. After harvesting potatoes my grandmother would boil some of the real small "new" potatoes and give me a bowl of them with butter on the top.

Here is her recipe for Rouladen and Potato Dumplings.

ROULADEN & POTATO DUMPLINGS

Thin round steak, pounded to tenderize. Cut into 2 1/2" x 4" strips.
mustard
onions
bacon

Spread strips of round steak with mustard. Lay slice of bacon (usually about a half of strip) in the center. Add sliced onions. Roll up and tie with sewing string or thread, so ingredients stay inside. Brown roll-ups on each side. Add water and simmer about 1 hour or more.

Ingredients for dumplings:

potatoes, cooked and mashed with no milk or butter added
flour
eggs

Mix cold mashed potatoes with 1 or 2 eggs (1 egg for 3 or 4 potatoes). Add enough flour so the potatoes can form a large roll. Roll the potatoes on a floured cutting board. The roll should be 1" in diameter. Cut into 1" pieces (my favorite job). Drop into boiling water. Take out with a slotted spoon when they rise to the top. Don't overcook. Drain them well or they will get gooey.

Serve with gravy, made from rouladen juices, and sauerkraut, over which more gravy is used.

From Loy Stutrud of McVille, North Dakota:

When my grandmother made this, she soaked the rice overnight and used chopped bacon or ham instead of pork. She used to bring this to picnics, wrapped in newspapers and a white dish towel.

HLUPRY, HULUPTURE, OR CABBAGE ROLLS

1 large head green cabbage
1 cup rice
1 onion, cut fine

1 lb. ground pork
salt & pepper, to taste
1 can sauerkraut

Steam the cabbage till the leaves can be rolled. Salt and pepper to taste. Mix the pork , onion, rice, and salt and pepper together. Take a leaf of the steamed cabbage and into it spread a tablespoon of the rice mixture and roll it up. Put a few torn leaves on the bottom of the kettle and put rolls in layers on top of leaves. Put a can of sauerkraut on top (you can use some of this on the bottom, too). Or use a can of sauerkraut juice. Then cover with water, boil 3 hours or till rice is done.

From Nancy Dirnbauer of Milwaukee, Wisconsin:

My paternal grandparents, Paul and Theresa Dirnbauer, came through Ellis Island in November 1907. They had sailed on the Carpathia from Purbach Am Neuseidler See in Austria, through Trieste, Italy, to New York. They were bound for Minnesota and finally settled in Milwaukee, Wisconsin.

HUNGARIAN BUTTER HORNS

4 cups all-purpose flour   1 1/4 cups butter
1/2 tsp. salt   3 egg yolks
1 tsp. vanilla   1/2 cup sour cream
1 oz. yeast

Sift flour, add salt, crumble yeast into flour. Mix butter into flour like pie dough, add beaten egg yolks, sour cream and vanilla. Mix well and knead.

<u>Filling</u>

Beat 3 egg whites until stiff
add 1 cup granulated sugar gradually
mix in 1/4 lb. (1 cup) finely chopped nuts
and 1 tsp. vanilla

Dredge board with powdered sugar instead of flour. Divide dough into 8 portions. Roll out thin and round as for pie. Cut into 8 wedges. Spread 1 teaspoon of filling on each wedge and roll toward center. Mold immediately and bake. Bake at 375° for 12 minutes.

Frost with powdered sugar frosting; makes 64.

From Buff Bethlen of New York City:

This recipe is from my maternal grandmother, Fani Hesser Pollak (1868-1957), who came from Hungary in 1907. I didn't realize how special the cookies were until I was the recipient of lavish praise from the teacher and other students when I served them at a school party. In Grandma's time, many hours were spent hand-grating the chocolate on a small grater and grinding the walnuts in a heavy brass mortar and pestle. Today, this can be done in minutes with the help of a food processor.

GRANDMA'S CHOCOLATE COOKIES

1/2 lb. semi-sweet chocolate, grated
1/2 lb walnuts, ground
1 cup sugar
2 eggs
1/4 tsp. ground cloves
a little bread crumbs or wheat germ
red cinnamon candy (hearts or dots)

Combine first five ingredients. Add enough bread crumbs or wheat germ to make mixture firm enough to handle. Roll into small balls. Flatten them on a greased cookie sheet. Press red cinnamon candy in center. Bake in slow oven (about 300°) for 20 minutes or until tops look baked. Let cool before removing.

From Maryanne Hansen of Bay Shore, New York:

My grandmother, Marie Psenitza Seidl, was born in Stampfen Pressbirger, Hungary. She arrived in the United States on September 20, 1905. She had seven children. My mother was the first born.

HAM AND NOODLE CASSEROLE

1 lb. egg noodles (break into small pieces before cooking)
2 eggs
4-6 cups left over ham (cut into very small pieces)
1 1/3 cups milk (approx.)
salt & pepper, to taste
bread crumbs
butter
paprika (optional)

Grease casserole with butter and sprinkle with bread crumbs. In a large bowl beat eggs, add milk and seasonings. Mix with cooked noodles and ham. Pour mixture into casserole dish. Sprinkle with bread crumbs. Dot with butter. Sprinkle with paprika, if desired. Bake at 350° until brown on top, about 1 hour.

From Debra Price Tula of Erin, Wisconsin:

Anton Harangozo came to the United States via Ellis Island in 1922, and in 1927, his wife, Ella, and daughter, Mary, were able to obtain their visas to come as well. Their hopes, as well as those of many others, was to escape communism. Knowing little English but with hard work, their dreams came true. This is dedicated to them and all the other immigrants who struggled to build our country. We love and miss you.

HUNGARIAN PLUM DUMPLINGS

12 medium Italian prune plums, pits out
2 cups sifted all-purpose flour
1 tsp. salt
6 tbsp. butter
2 cups cold mashed potatoes
2 eggs
3/4 cup dry bread crumbs
cinnamon

Sift flour and salt and cut in 3 tbsp. butter. Knead in potatoes, then eggs, until a smooth consistency. Roll out dough on to a well floured surface. Cut into 3" squares. Put plum in center. Sprinkle with cinnamon. Bring up ends and moisten with water to seal. With floured hands, press dough around plums firmly, pushing out air spaces. Cook in large kettle of boiling water. Don't crowd dumplings. Drain. Brown crumbs & butter. Add dumplings.

From Margaret Schmidt of Buffalo, New York:

My father came from Austria in 1901. My mother came from Hungary in 1902. They were married in Arad, Hungary, in 1889. She came with six children and no one could speak English.

APPLE BITTE
(MA'S APPLE DELIGHT)

2/3 cup vegetable shortening
2 egg yolks
1/2 cup sugar
1 1/2 tsp. baking powder
1 lemon, juice & rind
2 cups all-purpose flour (or as needed)
ground nuts (if desired)

Filling

3 large apples, grated
1/2 cup fine bread crumbs
juice of 1 lemon
1/2 to 1 cup sugar (to sweetness desired)
vanilla

Mix dough and put half in bottom of baking pan (not more than 1/2" thick). Mix filling and spread on dough. Top with balance of dough.

Topping

2 egg whites, beaten
1/4 lb. ground nuts

Spread beaten egg whites over top. Sprinkle nuts over all. Bake at 350° about 30 minutes or until done. Cut into bars.

From Margaret Sieg of Altamonte Springs, Florida:

My grandmother came through Ellis Island in the 1900's. She was the world's best cook in my opinion.

CHICKEN PAPRIKAS (PAPRIKAS CSIRKE)

1 onion, chopped
several carrots
celery
1 tbsp. paprika
1 tsp. black pepper

2 tsp. salt
4 or 5 lbs. chicken, white meat
2 1/2 cups water
1 pint sour cream
ketchup, to flavor

Put onions, carrots and celery in pan. Add water and seasonings. Put in chicken and let simmer slowly for about an hour until tender. Remove chicken, add sour cream to broth in pan and mix well. Add a little ketchup for flavor. You may serve in soup fashion adding noodles, or serve with chicken on the side.

From Mrs. Andrew W. Syposs of Tonawanda, New York:

My father-in-law came over here with his parents when he was eight months old in 1893, from Sajokaza, Borsod County, Hungary. This is an excellent recipe brought over by my husband's grandmother, translated and updated by the family. Geza and Mary Syposs arrived with their son, Andrew, on the S.S. Moravia on October 12, 1893, through Ellis Island.

LUSTA TORTA

1/2 lb. unsalted butter, softened
4 egg yolks
1 cup sugar
1 cup ground almonds
1/4 tsp. almond extract
1/2 cup rum
1/2 cup milk
3 pkgs. (48) lady fingers (sponge cakes)
1 cup heavy cream
2 tbsp. sugar
1 tsp. vanilla

Beat the butter in a mixer at high speed until light and fluffy. Beat together the egg yolks and sugar until very thick and lemon colored. Combine the egg yolks and sugar with the butter. Fold in the almonds and almond extract. Pour the rum and milk into a small bowl. Cut the lady fingers in half, lengthwise. Dip lady fingers briefly into rum and milk. Do not soak them in the liquid. Line bottom and sides of 8" or 9" cake pan with lady fingers. Cover with a layer of almond cream. Continue layering dipped lady fingers and almond cream until all are used. Top with a layer of lady fingers. Cover with a clean towel and weight the cake with a plate. Chill for 12 hours. Unmold the cake.

Whip the cream until slightly thickened. Add the sugar and vanilla and continue beating until cream is very thick. Spread the cream attractively over the top and sides of cake. Decorate the cake with strawberries. 10 to 12 servings.

From Ethel Dudas Stango of Toledo, Ohio:

I passed through Ellis Island in February 1929 at the age of seven with my mother. We came from Hungary.

WALNUT NOODLES

1/2 lb. ground walnuts
1/4 cup sugar

1 lb. noodles
2 tbsp. butter

Cook noodles in water with a little salt until done, drain well. Melt butter and while hot, pour over noodles and stir. Mix sugar and walnuts, add to noodles, mix well and serve hot. More sugar may be added if desired.

From Anne Boublis Ferriera of Glastonbury, Connecticut:

My mother arrived in the U.S.A. via Ellis Island from Lithuania in 1913. This is a favorite family recipe that she made for us through the years.

KUGELIS TARKE (POTATO PUDDING)

10 large potatoes
(use old, not new potatoes)
1 medium onion
5 slices salt pork
2 tbsp. farina (cream of wheat)
1/4 tsp. pepper
1/2 tsp. salt
1/2 cup hot milk
3 eggs

Peel and grate fine the potatoes and onion. Mince salt pork, fry till crisp. Pour fat and salt pork over potatoes. Add hot milk. Add beaten eggs, one at a time, salt and pepper, farina. Pour into greased pan (depth of potato mixture should be 2 - 2 1\2"). Bake at 400° for 15 minutes. Reduce heat to 375°. Bake 45 minutes longer. Serve hot, with sour cream -- as main course or side dish. Delicious!

From Justin Slepitis of Atlantic City, New Jersey:

My mother, Antoinette Bumblauskas, came from Lithuania to Ellis Island. She gave me this recipe.

BLEENIES AND KUGEL

6 large potatoes   1 tbsp. baking powder
1 large onion   2 tbsp. all-purpose flour
2 eggs   6 strips bacon (for top)
salt & pepper, to taste

Grate potatoes and onion. Add all ingredients and mix thoroughly.

For Kugel

Pour mixture into a greased baking pan or casserole dish 12" x 7"- put bacon on top. Bake in 400° oven until brown. Crust will form when bacon is crisp. Remove from pan and serve.

For Bleenies (Potato Pancakes)

Hot oil is necessary. Pour small amounts into pan of hot oil. Fry until brown.

Eat either one hot. May garnish with apple jelly or sour cream.

From Mrs. Pauline Tilton of Lakewood, New Jersey:

My mother came over in 1900 from Wilno, Lithuania, and the family was poor. Their staple was a lot of vegetables. She served this soup twice a week and other soups during the week. This is her soup. We called it sour-grass soup.

SORREL SOUP

2 quarts of chicken or beef stock
1 lb. sorrel
2 potatoes
4 tbsp. lard

4 egg yolks
4 oz. sour cream
salt & pepper, to taste

Clean sorrel, then <u>scald</u> with hot water, cut thin and fine. Cook in lard till tender. Cook potatoes, then cut sorrel and potatoes through sieve, mix well. Simmer 8 minutes. Beat egg yolks, add 2 tbsp. hot broth. Add into hot broth and heat. Spoon into bowls with a heaping tablespoon of sour cream and serve. 4 to 6 servings.

From Mrs. Higgins of New London, Connecticut:

The following recipe is a Lithuanian appetizer my mother would serve for Sunday breakfast.

1 smaltz (fat) herring, or, if you
 prefer, the leaner kind, cleaned
1 onion, thinly sliced
2 tbsp. salad oil

Soak cleaned herring overnight in cold water -- change water once or twice. Next day, place wiped fish in baking pan. Overlap onions from head to tail. Trickle salad oil over all. Bake in 350° oven till golden (15 minutes). Serve with scrambled eggs and plenty of coffee.

From Irena Konczak Pentz of Johnstown, Pennsylvania:

My father, Stefan Konczak, emigrated to the United States via Ellis Island in 1913 from Poznan, Poland. He owned a photography and printing business and led his own orchestra, playing clarinet and saxophone. He later became the proprietor of a liquor establishment. There are four generations of musicians in the family.

This recipe was handed down by my babusia (grandmother). In our home it is traditional, served only on Easter Sunday, symbolizing the culmination of the Lenten fast. Holy Week services left little time for the preparation of a many-coursed dinner, and everyone looked forward to this hearty meat-filled dish after singing the final strains of "Chrystus zmartwychwstal jest."

BIALY BARSZCZ WIELKANOCNA (WHITE EASTER BARSZCZ)

2 lbs. Polish butcher shop smoked kielbasa
Approx. 10 cups of cold water
4 tbsp. white vinegar
4-5 tbsp. all-purpose flour, made into paste with water
4 eggs, slightly whisked
1/2 pint light sweet cream
salt & pepper, to taste

Serve with potatoes, ham, kielbasa and hard-boiled eggs.

Wash kielbasa. In a large pot, bring kielbasa in water to a full boil. Reduce heat and simmer for 20 to 25 minutes. Turn off heat and allow meat to rest in water for 20 minutes. Remove to platter. Reheat stock. Add vinegar and then the flour which has been made into a paste with 6 or more tbsp. cold water, stirring into stock, which will slightly thicken it. Whisk the eggs in a quart size bowl and blend in the sweet cream. Ladle some of the hot stock into the egg and cream mixture stirring constantly so as to temper it. Return this mixture into stock, stirring constantly to prevent curdling.

Optional: saute chopped onion in butter in a large skillet and add to cubed parboiled potatoes, working potatoes through the onions.

Remove to serving dish. On separate dishes, place small chunks or pieces of warm baked ham, thinly sliced kielbasa, and cut-up hard boiled eggs.

Into wide soup bowls, ladle barszcz. Each can then spoon into center the potatoes, adding the ham, kielbasa and eggs as much as they desire. If you have white home-ground horseradish, a small teaspoon adds to the flavor.

From Mrs. M.J. Olejnik of Lackawanna, New York:

My grandmother, Mary Bobonski Skubik, came to the United States via Ellis Island. She was born in Poland and came here as a young girl. She met my grandfather, Stanley, in Lackawanna, New York. They married and settled here.

CHRUSCIKI

12 eggs yolks
1 tbsp. melted butter
1 cup sour cream
1 tbsp. confectioners' sugar
4 to 5 cups all-purpose flour
1 shot of whiskey (approx. 1 1/2 oz.)

Beat egg yolks with all ingredients except the flour. Add the flour slowly, using just enough to make a noodle-like dough. Roll the dough on a lightly floured board until very thin. Cut the dough into rectangles. Cut a slit in center of each rectangle. Pull one corner through the slit to make a sort of bow-tie. Fry in hot melted lard until lightly browned. Drain on absorbent paper. Cool and dust with confectioners' sugar.

Enjoy !

From Antoinette De Lancey of Wilmington, Delaware:

I am enclosing one recipe used by my mother, an excellent cook, who acquired the recipe by observing my grandmother, an immigrant from Poland.

The recipe, "Zur or Sour Dough Soup," is just scrumptious in my opinion. You have to prepare the sour dough juice first. My mother used to get the sour dough or flour from a Polish bakery.

When I was a child, my family referred to it by another name; however, I recently found out that "Zur" soup was its correct name.

ZUR SOUP OR SOUR DOUGH SOUP

Zur juice

2 cups coarse rye flour
4 cups warm water
1 tbsp. leavening or crust of rye bread
3 cloves garlic

Place flour in jar. Combine with part of water. Add leavening or crust and crushed garlic and mix. When emulsion settles add water 3 inches off top of flour. Cover with perforated paper or cloth and set aside in warm place 3 days.

Soup

3 cups water drained from cooked potatoes
1/2 lb sausage
2 cups sour juice (zur)
salt
2 cloves garlic
2 tbsp. cut bacon fat, or 3-4 strips bacon, cut

Drain water, brought to boil. Add cut sausage, add sour juice. Bring to boil. Add garlic. Before serving, add potatoes and bacon.

From Alice H. Tiede Anderson of Winneconne, Wisconsin:

PIEROGI

Serve as dessert or lunch.

2 containers <u>dry</u> cheese	1 container sour cream
4 eggs, separated	2/3 cup all-purpose flour
4 tbsp. sugar	1/2 tsp. salt
2 tbsp. butter, soft	1 stick unsalted butter
1/4 tsp. cinnamon	1/2 cup dry bread crumbs

With the back of a spoon or grater, rub cheese through a medium metal fine sieve (drainer). Beat in egg yolks, one at a time, then the sugar and softened butter. Sift the flour over the cheese mixture. Stir vigorously till flour is absorbed. In a mixing bowl beat egg whites <u>till stiff</u>. Scoop whites over the cheese mixture and fold gently but thoroughly. On slightly floured surface, roll small rolls 1" diameter by 12" long, flatten slightly and cut crosswise into six 2" rounds. In a 3 to 4 quart pot bring 2 quarts salted water to a boil. Drop 6 dumplings into water, stirring gently so not to stick on bottom. Reduce heat to low and poach dumplings for 5 minutes, or until they feel firm when prodded gently with finger. With slotted spoon transfer dumplings into a colander to drain. Cover them loosely in another pot to keep warm while poaching the remainder. In an 8" skillet melt butter, do not let brown, add bread crumbs and fry till crisp and golden brown. Remove from heat.

<u>To serve</u>

Arrange dumplings on a <u>heated</u> platter. Pour browned bread crumbs on top. Top with dollops of sour cream. Sprinkle with white sugar and cinnamon to taste.

Enjoy!!

From Dorothy D. Bembenista of Buffalo, New York:

This recipe has nourished our families for two generations. This was basically a simple, fast, nourishing food that warmed the hearts and filled the stomachs of my three sons after coming home from active outdoor play in the cold. We are of Polish descent, but I'm sure the origin of this food is known to many people of various ethnic heritages.

ZACIERKI

1 large egg
1 cup all-purpose flour
1/4 tsp. salt

Mix with fork until resembles course meal. Crumble loosely into 2 cups boiling water. Add 1/2 tsp. salt and cook on low heat 2 minutes. Top each serving with pat of butter and add warm milk. Serves 4.

From Patricia C. Abramoski of Amherst, New York:

My husband's grandmother, Constance Rzodkiewicz, came through Ellis Island from Poland and was detained there for three months in 1908 along with his mother, who was only two years old then. His mother, Sophie Rzodkiewicz Abramoski, had gotten a rash on the way over and the officials feared she had smallpox. They shaved her head and scrubbed her down and frightened poor Grandma who spoke no English.

This is the recipe Grandma brought with her and continued to make until she was too old.

SPARERIBS, CABBAGE & SAUERKRAUT

3-4 lbs. of spare ribs
 (soak in water 1/2 hour & drain)
1 large can sauerkraut
 (reserve liquid, add water to make two cups)
 (rinse sauerkraut well 3 or 4 times)
4-5 quarts of water
3-4 bay leaves
4-5 whole peppercorns
1 small onion, quartered

Cook 1 1/2 hours.

Add 1 medium head of shredded cabbage and cook another hour.

In frying pan on <u>medium</u> heat add:

4 tbsp. of lard or butter
4 tbsp. of all-purpose flour

Mix until golden brown.

Gradually add 2 cups of sauerkraut liquid to this mix. Add this to the pot of sauerkraut and mix well. Cook 1/2 hour and serve with plain boiled potatoes or mashed potatoes.

From Janit Romayko of East Hartford, Connecticut:

APOLONIA'S POLISH HONEY CAKE

1/2 cup shortening
2 egg yolks
1 cup sugar
1 whole egg
1 pound honey
3 1/2 cups all-purpose flour
1 tsp. salt

1/2 tsp. ginger
2 tsp. baking powder
1 tsp. baking soda
1 tsp. allspice
1 cup coffee
2 eggs, (whites, beaten stiffly)

Cream shortening and sugar. Add egg yolks, whole egg, and honey. Add rest of dry ingredients with coffee. When well mixed, fold in egg whites. Bake in 350° oven in well-greased tube pan, 50 minutes or until done.

From Judith Walsh of Brooklyn, New York:

My father's mother, Esther Wolkowich, was born in a small town in the Russian sector of Poland. She came to the United States at the turn of the century and brought some native recipes with her. My favorite was her matzoh meal pancakes recipe.

Every Passover, with her admiring grandchildren standing around her, she held sway over her bowl of matzoh meal mixture and the frying pan, turning out the mouth-watering pancakes by the dozen. It was a Passover highlight. We ate them as fast as she could make them.

GRANDMA'S MATZOH MEAL PANCAKES

1/2 cup matzoh meal
1/2 tsp. salt
3/4 tbsp. sugar
3/4 cup cold water
3 eggs
oil for frying

Combine matzoh meal, salt and sugar. Separate eggs. Beat yolks slightly and combine with water. Add liquids with dry ingredients. Beat egg whites until stiff and fold into matzoh meal mixture. Heat oil in frying pan. Drop mixture by tablespoon into hot oil. Brown pancakes on both sides.

Ingredients can be doubled or tripled as desired. Should be served immediately for best taste. Can be served with powdered sugar, jam or any other topping, or served without topping. Makes 10 - 12.

From Regina Gold Sussman of Lake Worth, Florida:

My parents were born in Lodz, Poland, and came to the U.S.A. at the turn of the century, having entered through Ellis Island, enduring trying entrance procedures. Two sons arrived with them, and about nine or ten years later, my sister and I completed the family scene. We grew up in difficult times, including two World Wars and the Great Depression. My father was a silk weaver, and his earnings were in the low-income level, and we had to learn to be thrifty in all areas of life. My mother therefore cooked foods that were nourishing but always kept in mind that they needed to cost as little as possible. Although we were "poor" financially, we did not feel deprived, the main reason being that we always enjoyed such good food.

POOR MAN'S LIVER SOUP (URREMA LABER ZUP)

flour (quantity equivalent in creating a white sauce)
butter (sufficient to absorb the flour)
salt & pepper, to taste

Combine the above in a skillet and brown as you would for making brown gravy. Add boiling water while mixing until smooth and creamy until it reaches the consistency of a creamed soup. Serve only with medium-size noodles, or kloiskalach.

PURIM CREPES (FRITLACH)

flour (about 2 tbsp. per crepe)   eggs (1 per 2 crepes)

Mix well and pour mixture to spread very thinly into a small frying pan in very hot peanut oil. When bubbles appear, the crepe should be finished and crispy. Sprinkle with powdered sugar.

SPINACH CUTLETS

spinach   matzoh meal or bread crumbs
eggs

Beat eggs. Mix together with cooked spinach and matzoh meal and form into cutlets. Fry in butter until brown on both sides.

This was very often served in the evening with garden salad. The usual meat and potatoes were usually served at midday as my father came home for lunch and needed a substantial meal to carry him through the day.

From Bernice Walters of Hillsboro, Illinois:

This is a simple recipe -- often prepared by my Polish mother-in-law, Clara Novak Walters, and often enjoyed by our family.

Many times she related to me her experiences in the early 1900's as a young woman: her marriage in Germany, her trip alone to America (her young husband, who had the wander-lust, had preceded her to America via Australia), disembarking at Ellis Island and traveling to the coal towns of Pennsylvania, where she and her husband John first settled. From there they moved to West Virginia, then to Colorado, and finally to Panama, Illinois, a small mining town in the south central part of the state, where they lived out their lives. They had four children, two girls and two boys, one of whom is my husband, Frank.

Our daughter gave birth recently to twin girls. For these babies, I wish a lifetime of happiness and fulfillment. I also hope that they and their three-year old brother will someday know how fortunate they are that their great-grandparents had the courage and the daring to leave all that was dear to them behind to seek a better life in America. I want our children - Janet, Betty, and David - to remember their heritage and to know the tremendous changes in life style, the hardships their grandparents endured, and the culture they brought to this country.

The family name was, of course, not Walters to begin with. My father-in-law's name was Lamparski, which he changed at some time after he arrived in America.

POTATO KLUSKI

Peel and boil 5 or 6 small potatoes. Mash and set aside to cool. Add 1 egg and enough flour to make the dough easy to handle. Roll out into rolls about 1 1/2" in diameter. Cut into 1" kluski (dumplings). Bring large pot of water to a rolling boil. Carefully drop kluski into water -- one at a time. When they are done, they will float to the top (they cook in only a few minutes). Remove from water with slotted spoon or spatula. Place in single layer on platter. Serve warm with roast beef or roast pork and gravy.

From Debra Jambor of Arlington, Texas:

My grandmother came to Ellis Island in November 1922 from Bessarabia, which is now called Moldavia, which is sometimes part of Romania and sometimes part of Russia. My grandmother considered herself Romanian.

She started a blintz factory with her husband, Eli Goldfarb, in Harris, New York, and introduced the first frozen blintzes to America!

My grandmother made cheese, blueberry, and cherry blintzes. She also specialized in strudel and knishes. Her name was Beatrice Goldfarb.

LEAF (BLETEL)

1 cup water
3/4 cup all-purpose flour
1/4 tsp. baking powder
3 eggs
2 tbsp. oil

Cheese Filling

1 pkg. farmers cheese
sugar, sweeten to taste (1 tsp. to 1 tbsp. approx.)

Mix water, flour, baking powder in one bowl, mix eggs and oil in another bowl and beat with mixer until well blended. Add egg mixture to the first bowl. If there are any lumps, put through a strainer.

Prepare Leaves

Grease 10" pan well. In medium-hot pan, pour 3/4 soup ladle of mixture slowly while rotating pan in air so mixture spreads evenly into paper-thin pancake covering the bottom of the pan. Cook 1-2 minutes until edges curl up making it easy to remove leaf. Use gloves to remove hot leaves or shake out cooked side up onto wax paper on a towel. My grandmother used a metal scoop shaped like a rectangle to put cheese (1" scoop) in from top edge. Fold top edge over cheese. Fold sides in, covering partially the top. Roll top down to form blintz. Cook blintzes in oil or butter until brown on both sides, turning to cook sides also. Serve hot with sour cream. Sour cream may also be sweetened with honey, if you prefer. Leaves can be prepared ahead of time and kept in refrigerator, or frozen for later use.

From Hallie Morrison Block of Buffalo, New York:

Jennie Greenfield Morrison arrived in Buffalo, New York, from Romania towards the end of the nineteenth century at the age of seventeen. Her father dealt in raw lumber in the small town which she pronounced "Puddle-oye." Jennie Greenfield was alone, and worked as a seamstress, doing hand-sewing. She joined a group of other Rumanians and met Jacob Morrison, who, as a tinsmith in Bucharest, was named Yankel Lupu.

They married and had an enduring, but not especially happy, marriage and raised six children. Jake originally worked to repair fenders. The family story is that he boarded streetcars to hand-deliver completed fenders to their owners. At the time of his death in 1952, Grandpa had built a prosperous business making steel-stampings -- truck bodies, garage doors, furnaces, etc.

Grandma Jennie was a marvelous cook. I still remember her stretching tissue-paper-thin strudel dough over a long table. Unfortunately, as with everything she made, there were no recipes, and most of her mouth-watering concoctions have disappeared into oblivion. There's one recipe I have managed to glean, however. I'll give you two ways to make it -- her way and my less time-consuming way. She called it "Puddle Jelly" (not to be confused with her town of "Puddle-oye), and it served my father and me, the only ones in my immediate family who loved it, as entree, salad, and dessert. It stood alone!

JENNIE GREENFIELD MORRISON'S PUDDLE JELLY

1 large eggplant, pricked many times with a fork
2 medium tomatoes
6 radishes
2 scallions
1 cucumber
1/4 - 1/3 cup of corn oil
salt, to taste (it takes LOTS of salt!)

Place eggplant in a large pot with a small amount of water. Cover and steam until the eggplant is soft. When eggplant is cool enough to handle, slit the skin and put eggplant meat into a large, wood chopping bowl. Chop with metal and wood chopper until no lumps remain. Add salad oil. Refrigerate. Dice the tomatoes and slice the other vegetables.

To serve: Present the eggplant and the other vegetables in separate bowls. Each person helps himself to some of each -- enough to almost cover a dinner plate, and then shakes and shakes and shakes salt till it tastes wonderful!

Here is my modernized version, with the same ingredients:

Pierce the eggplant all over. Place in covered microwave dish with 1/4 cup of water. "Nuke" the eggplant on high speed 12-15 minutes, or until tender. When eggplant is cool enough to handle, slit the skin and put eggplant meat in food processor. Process with on/off mode, or use "pulse" setting until lumps no longer remain. Add salad oil and process for a very short time. The vegetables may be sliced by hand or in the processor.

Serve just as Grandma did.

From Doris Abrams Granad of Houston, Texas:

This is my mother's recipe. Her name was Mrs. Nettie Schwartz Abrams. Mother came to America by way of Ellis Island in 1898. She was twelve years old when she came to America from Romania. She came here with her parents, Aaron and Golda Schwartz, and her brother, Adolph. They were a Jewish family that came to beautiful America to escape religious oppression.

POTLAGELA (EGGPLANT SALAD)

1 medium-size eggplant
1 large onion, cut in large chunks after peeling
1/4 cup of corn oil or olive oil
salt & pepper, to taste

Fry the onion in oil till golden brown. Place eggplant in a foil covered pan. Bake uncovered at 350° till eggplant is soft. Peel and throw away the skin and stem. Mash in a bowl. Add fried onions and the oil. Salt and pepper. Cover, refrigerate and serve over a bed of lettuce, tomatoes and black greek olives.

Oh, so good!

From Julia G. Van Der Meer Of Yardley, Pennsylvania

My parents, not then married, came here from Romania through Ellis Island.

I always remember us eating bacon bread or, as my daughters called it, "Dirty Bread". My mother would buy a piece of bacon, thick and meatless. Then she would get very hearty round brown bread and slice it thick. Then put sliced onions and tomatoes over it. Out in the yard she would build a fire, put the bacon on a long stick and let it melt and put the bacon drippings over the bread and stuff.

Mmmm, was this good! We thought we had died and gone to heaven!

From Clarlyn Bychok of Dallas, Texas:

My mother-in-law came by herself at age sixteen from Onufrovichi, Russia, and landed at Ellis Island in 1916. Her older brother, Feodor, had come a few years earlier to Windsor, Vermont. He sent passage money for her older sister Christina to come to America. The sister did not want to leave Russia and the younger sister, Tatiana "Tina" Borisova Pesarik, came instead of Christina. The brother returned to Russia soon after Tina arrived when he learned of the death of his small daughter in Russia. Before leaving, Feodor "arranged" for the marriage of his sister Tatiana to another Russian immigrant, Michael Bychok. They were married in the Russian Orthodox Church in Claremont, New Hampshire, in 1918. Tina often made these pastries for her grandchildren who thought they were wonderful treats to eat. Since none of the six grandchildren spoke Russian, they had difficulty calling them by the Russian name, so they renamed them "Twisters." In the area of White Russia near Minsk where her family had lived, Tina said these pastries were always served at the village church after a wedding or funeral or on very special occasions.

HARUSCHEE

2 cups all-purpose flour
1/3 cup sugar
3 eggs
1/2 tsp. almond flavoring
oil

Mix sugar and eggs together in mixing bowl. Add about 2 cups flour (depending on size of eggs). Add almond flavoring. Roll out paper thin (the thinner the better). Cut into rectangles about 1-1/2" x 5" and make a 2" slit longways in each pastry strip. Pull one end of strip through slit to make a "bow tie." Fry a few at a time in medium hot deep fat until lightly colored. They will float to top when about ready to be turned. Turn only once. When ready, remove from hot oil and drain on paper towels. Sprinkle on both sides with sugar or sifted powdered sugar while still warm. The thinner the dough is rolled, the crisper the pastries will be.

BULKA

1 pkg. yeast (1/4 oz.)
1 tsp. sugar
1/4 lb. butter
1/2 cup sugar
1 cup milk
pinch salt
1 tsp. almond extract

4-5 cups all-purpose flour, sifted
4 eggs
2 tbsp. (or more) cinnamon
1/2 cup sugar
white raisins, if desired

Disolve yeast in 1/4 cup warm water plus 1 tsp. sugar. Set aside for yeast to grow. In sauce pan combine and heat butter, 1/2 cup sugar, milk, salt and almond extract until butter and sugar are melted.

Cool the mixture to room temperature. Beat 4 eggs in mixing bowl. Add 1 cup flour and yeast mixture. Add 3-4 cups flour, alternating with milk and butter mixture which has been cooled to room temperature. (Do not add milk when hot or yeast will not grow.) Cover dough in mixing bowl and let rise until double in bulk. Knead dough on lightly floured board and let rise again. Turn out on board and knead a second time. Roll dough to about 1/2 inch thickness. Cover with a thin coating of soft butter, then sprinkle with a mixture of 1/2 cup sugar and 2 tbsp. (or more) of cinnamon. Add white raisins if desired. Roll up as for jelly roll. Cut into 6 sections and place these one at a time, slightly overlapping each, in a greased tube pan or angel food cake tin. Bake at 350° for 50-60 minutes or until lightly browned on top. Remove from oven and let stand 10 minutes before turning out of pan. Turn bread upright. When cooled, frost top with confectioners' icing and let frosting drizzle down sides. While frosting is still soft, sprinkle with multi-colored sugar sprinkles.

Traditionally, this was served at the end of the meal with butter and cream cheese.

From Marian Burros of New York, New York:

This is a recipe of my mother, Dorothy Derby Fox Greenblatt, who arrived at Ellis Island from the Ukraine on November 20, 1906. This is a typical Russian-Jewish recipe and was always a family favorite.

ROLLED CABBAGE

1 medium head cabbage	brown sugar
1 lb. lean ground beef	lemon juice
1 medium onion, finely chopped	1/2 - 3/4 cup raisins
1 sliced onion	salt
1 can whole tomatoes (1 lb.)	

Boil head of cabbage until soft, 15-30 minutes. Cool, core, and remove leaves carefully.   Combine and mix thoroughly meat and chopped onion.   Place small amount of meat in leaf and roll.

In pot, place cabbage rolls with sliced onion, tomatoes, sugar, lemon, raisins, and salt. Sugar and lemon amounts vary on individual taste, so frequent tasting is necessary. Simmer, covered, very slowly for 2 hours. Refrigerate or freeze. When ready to serve, return to room temperature, place in shallow pan in oven for 1/2 hour at 350°. Baste often and brown well. Adjust seasoning if necessary. 4-6 servings.

From Mary Veehoff of Storm Lake, Iowa:

My parents came from the Ukraine in 1912 to the new country. They farmed and raised thirteen children, of which I am the youngest.

My mother loved to cook, and I still make her favorite recipes, which my family enjoys.

BEET SOUP (BORSH)

2 cups beets, cut into thin strips
1/2 cup carrots, cut into strips
1 medium onion, chopped
1 medium potato, small cubes
1 tsp. dill weed
1 tsp. parsley, chopped fine

2 cups shredded cabbage
1/2 cup fresh or frozen peas
9 cups water
2 tbsp. lemon juice or vinegar
1 1/2 tsp. salt
1/2 cup sour or sweet cream

Cover beets and carrots with water, add lemon juice and salt and simmer 1/2 hour. Add rest of vegetables. Cook 1/2 hour longer and pour cream and serve.

JELLIED PIGS FEET (STUDENETZ)

2 pigs feet, cut lengthwise
1 pork hock
celery stalk
1 tbsp. salt
2 cloves garlic
1 bay leaf

Scrape, trim and wash thoroughly. Place the meat, celery, salt and garlic in a large kettle, cover with cold water and bring to a boil. Turn heat down and simmer slowly. Rapid boiling will make the broth milky. Cook until bones fall apart. Takes 3-4 hours. Turn heat off. Add crushed garlic, cool. Remove all bones, cut up meat, arrange in a dish. Season with salt and pepper. Strain juice over meat. Chill until firm. Serve.

From Shirley E. Greenwald of New York, New York:

My Aunt Sarah came from Russia in the early 1900's. She passed through Ellis Island on her way to Brooklyn. Some years ago, we made sure to watch her cook this recipe and measure the ingredients as she went along and made our modifications for easy preparation.

AUNT SARAH'S UNSTUFFED STUFFED CABBAGE

1 head cabbage (2 lbs.)
1 medium onion, diced
1 can tomatoes (1 lb. 12 oz.)

Wash, quarter, shred head of cabbage and arrange in bottom of deep pot with cover. Add onion and tomatoes. Top with meatballs made by mixing:

1 lb. chopped beef or ground turkey
1/2 tsp. each salt & sugar
1 tbsp. ketchup
pepper, freshly ground

Add enough tomato juice to cover cabbage and meat.

Add:

juice of 1/2 lemon
1 tsp. sugar
4-5 ginger snaps, crumbled

Cover and simmer 1-2 hours, stirring from time to time. Best when cooked ahead and reheated. Serves 4-6. Double recipe for a crowd.

From Mrs. Eva Effron Acker Goldin of Poughkeepsie, New York:

Momma Effron came from Grodno, Russia, in 1901, landing at Ellis Island. Herring in a jar (8 ounces) may be substituted for the matjes herring. In Momma's day, herring came in wooden barrels (small size) or wooden tubs.

MAMMA FANNY LABENSKY EFFRON'S CHOPPED HERRING

1 matjes herring, soaked over night, skinned and cut into pieces
1 medium-size onion
1 large, fairly sour apple
2 hard-boiled eggs
1 slice of toasted challah
1/2 cup vinegar
3 tbsp. salad oil
2 tbsp. sugar
1 tsp. salt
1/4 tsp. fresh ground pepper

Put through a hand grinder, then chop in a wooden bowl till well mixed. Serve with crackers or matzos.

From Josephine Eckman of Bismarck, North Dakota:

Here are several recipes from our Germans-from-Russia ancestors. They were Germans that went to Russia in the early 1800's and then came to America, landing on Ellis Island in the early 1900's.

Many of the German-Russians were poor immigrants. They served many dough recipes when meat was scarce.

All these grandparents were farmers. They made the Dakota prairie blossom and eked out a living in spite of drought, hail, and the hot summer sun. Their lives evolved around their church and family. Close bonds exist among all the family yet today in spite of the miles that separate the clan. Most try to have an annual reunion or get together and celebrate with a meal and dance following a wedding.

Johannes and Elizabeth Diegel and their seven-month old daughter, Christine, left Hoffnungstal, Russia, to go to Wishek, North Dakota. They sailed on the Columbia and arrived in New York on November 28, 1905. They were farmers. They were blessed with fourteen children.

WASSERMELON & NUDLA
(WATERMELON & DUMPLINGS)

2 cups all-purpose flour	3/4 cup milk
1 1/2 tsp. salt	1 1/2 cups water
2 tsp. baking powder	2 tbsp. shortening
2 eggs	1 medium potato, sliced

Ready two heavy 9" skillets by pouring water, salt, shortening and potato in them. Bring to a boil and drop the dumpling mixture (rest of ingredients) by teaspoons. Cover and do not peek until you hear them sizzling and they smell done (15 minutes or so). Serve with watermelon slices.

Dumplings were also often served with onion sauce.

ONION SAUCE

Brown 1/4 cup flour in 3 tbsp. lard. Add 1 large onion, 1 tsp. salt, 2 tsp. sugar, 1 1/2 tsp. vinegar. Add 1 1/2 cups water. Simmer until onions are tender.

GERMAN KUCHEN (COFFEE CAKE)

<u>Dough</u>

1 pkg. active dry yeast (1/4 oz.)
1 cup warm water
1/2 cup oil
1/2 cup sugar
2 tsp. salt
1 cup warm milk
7 cups all-purpose flour

<u>Custard topping</u>

2 cups cream
3 eggs
1 cup sugar
1 cup milk
2 tbsp. all-purpose flour
fruit, sliced
cinnamon
sugar

Dissolve yeast in water for 5 minutes. Mix sugar, salt, oil and warm milk. Add flour and yeast mixture. Knead and let rise. Punch down. Roll out into pie shape and put on bottom of pie pan. Top with sliced fruit and custard topping. Sprinkle cinnamon and sugar on top. Bake 350° for 20 minutes.

Note: Dough should be rolled thin like a pie crust. Remaining dough can be frozen. Makes about six or seven cakes.

From Rena Weinstein of East Northport, New York:

This is my grandmother's wonderful noodle pudding recipe. She passed through Ellis Island in the early years of this century and is still a joy to us today at age ninety-four.

GRANDMA CELIA'S NOODLE PUDDING

1 stick butter
1 lb. medium egg noodles, cooked
4 eggs, separated
1/2 pint sour cream
1 lb. pot cheese
1/2 cup milk
1 lb. can crushed pineapples (a recent addition)
3/4 cup sugar

Preheat oven to 360°. Melt butter in baking pan. Beat egg yolks. Add sugar gradually. Add sour cream, pot cheese, milk, pineapple, and melted butter. Pour over cooked noodles and combine.

Beat egg whites until stiff and carefully fold into egg yolk mixture. Turn into greased rectangular baking dish, about 10" x 13". Set in oven and bake 1 1/2 hours or until firm and brown on top. Makes 8 - 10 servings.

From Hermine Dicke of Madison, Wisconsin:

My parents, Marie and John Prisland, came to America through Ellis Island from Slovenia. My mother was an outstanding leader among the Slovenian women in the United States, having founded the Slovenian Women's Union of America in 1926.

AJMPREN CUCUMBERS

2 medium cucumbers	2 tbsp. all-purpose flour
1 tbsp. salt	1 1/2 cups potato broth
4 medium potatoes	(cracklings (ocvrki), if desired)
2 cups water	1 tsp. vinegar
1 tsp. salt	1/4 tsp. pepper
2 tbsp. lard	1/4 pound bacon, fried until crisp

Peel cucumbers and slice paper thin into a bowl. Mix in the tbsp. salt and set aside for at least 1 hour. Peel the potatoes and cook in 2 cups water and 1 tsp. salt. When tender, drain, reserve potato broth and mash.

Roux (Ajmpren):

In a heavy skillet heat the lard. Add flour, stirring constantly, and cook over low heat until golden brown. Gradually stir in 1 1/2 cups potato broth. (If cracklings are desired, add now). Add the cucumbers that have been thoroughly squeezed with hands to remove all liquid. Stir in the vinegar and cook for 7 minutes. Add the mashed potatoes to the mixture until well blended. Place in serving dish and sprinkle with 1/4 tsp. pepper. Garnish with crumbled bacon. This can be served as a main meal or side dish.

As children, we were sometimes served a bowl of vegetable or milk soup with it.

From Stacia Anderson Kirby of Seattle, Washington:

This recipe has been a family favorite for three generations. My grandmother, Rose Klarich Weller, made this recipe often since it is good, cheap, and warms you on a cold day in the Northwest. Rose came through Ellis Island in 1920 from Yugoslavia. She arrived with her mother, Katherine, and brother Marion. My great-grandfather had already arrived in the States three years earlier. He took the railroad across the country to Tacoma, Washington, where he worked as a lumberjacker. He sent his money home to bring his family over to America.

JECHMIK SOUP

1 meaty ham bone or 2 ham hocks (about 2-3 lbs.)
1/2 cup slightly chopped celery
1 large onion, chopped
2 carrots, sliced
2 bay leaves
1/2 tsp. oregano, dried, not ground
1/2 tsp. marjoram, dried, not ground
2 tbsp. fresh parsley (1 tbsp. dried)
2 cloves garlic, slivered
1/2 cup barley
3/4 cup canned red kidney beans
1 1/2 cup milk
1 cup chopped ham or sausage
pepper, to taste

There is no need to add salt, as the ham adds enough of that.

In a large simmering pot, cover ham with enough water to cover generously. Add onion, celery, carrot, spices and garlic. Simmer for 2-3 hours. Remove bones and skim broth for fat. Add barley and simmer 1 hour covered. Add milk, beans, ham and pepper to taste. Cook about 10 minutes longer and serve. Makes 8-10 servings.

From Barbara Kucan of Monroeville, Pennsylvania:

My mother-in-law, Ann Kucan, was born in Zagreb, Yugoslavia, in 1913 and came to the United States as a child.

STRUDEL

This recipe makes 5-6 pie plates of strudel.

Dough:

1 1/2 sticks butter, melted
2 eggs
1 tsp. salt
2 cups warm water
6 cups all-purpose flour

Mix first 4 ingredients. Add flour, a little at a time, until well-mixed. More flour may be added until dough is no longer sticky. Knead dough a little by hand, until not sticky. Cut dough into 2 pieces. Butter 2 plates. Put dough on plates and cover with warm bowls. Let dough rest for 1 hour. After dough rests, roll out to a large circle. Cover with cloth and let it rest 10 minutes. Stretch dough over table. Dough will be paper-thin. Cut off thick edges. Let dough dry for 5-10 minutes.

Filling:

2 bags of MacIntosh apples, peeled and sliced thin
2 1/2 - 2 3/4 cups sugar
cinnamon
2 sticks butter, melted

Use half of the filling for the first piece of dough, the rest for the second piece of dough.

Spread apples on half of dough. Sprinkle sugar and cinnamon over all dough. Drip butter all over. Flip up hanging side over apples. Add a few more apples, sugar, cinnamon, and butter. Begin rolling from apple side. When hanging edges come over table, sprinkle with sugar and butter. Roll to the end. Shape into pie plates. Cover open ends with extra dough from ends. Bake at 375° for 15 minutes, then 350° for 1/2 hour to 45 minutes, or until done. To freeze: Cover unbaked strudel with plastic wrap, then foil. When baking, remove wrapppings and bake longer.

From Carol M. Rapson of East Lansing, Michigan:

My grandmother, Frances Belian Chopp, arrived by herself when she was fifteen in 1901 from Yugoslavia. She spoke no English, and when she arrived, they put a sign around her neck to catch a train for the upper Michigan Copper Country. They gave her a banana, but she did not know what to do with it, as she had never seen a banana before. She watched, and when others peeled and ate the banana, she did the same.

FILENA ZELIA (CABBAGE ROLLS)

3 lbs. ground ham
1/2 cup regular rice, washed
1 large cabbage
2 jars sauerkraut
pepper

Cut core out of cabbage; cover with boiling water and boil until outer leaves are soft. Mix ham and rice. Roll meat mixture into cabbage leaves. Place layer of sauerkraut on the bottom of large pan and place filled cabbage leaves; when bottom of pan is covered, place layer of sauerkraut over cabbage leaves. Continue until all ingredients are used. Pepper to taste, cover with boiling water and simmer gently for 2 hours. Serve with boiled potatoes.

From Dorothy and Jacob Schwaner of Oceanside, California:

My husband's mother and father both passed through Ellis Island. This is her recipe for Kartoffel Schussel (Potato Dish). We know little of her ancestry except that her maiden name was Wilhelmina Kittleberger; her father was Adam Kittleberger; her mother, Minnie Mallaner. She was born in Yugoslavia. She married Ferdinand Schwaner, native of Austria-Hungary, in Ohio. Her brother sent her the money to come over to America, and after landing at Ellis Island, she took the train to Mansfield, Ohio, where her brother lived. When she arrived there no one met her, and she finally found a man pushing a cart that spoke her language, and he took her to her brother's house. She got a job in a cigar factory making $1.50 a week and paid her brother back. She arrived in 1908 and was sixteen years old at that time. She raised four children and never went back to Europe.

KARTOFFEL SCHUSSEL

6 large potatoes, peeled
1 large onion, chopped
1 large parsnip, chopped
3 bay leaves
6 peppercorns
1/2 tsp. salt
1/2 cup tomato juice

all-purpose flour, small amount
2 tbsp. sour cream
dash vinegar, if desired

Cover the first group of ingredients above with water and cook until potatoes are done. Drain off the water. Thicken a bit with small amount of flour and water and then add 2 tbsp. sour cream and serve. This is a good side dish especially good with sausage. You can add a dash of vinegar if desired. Serves 4.

From Mrs. Frank Suprina of Seaford, New York:

*My husband, who came to this country from Yugoslavia at age fourteen, often
told the story of when he and the other young men he traveled with arrived at
Ellis Island. They were sold a "Box Lunch" for one dollar. In it was a sandwich
and a banana which none of the boys had ever seen before. The boys were told by
the workers to eat the skin and throw away the inside. They very quickly learned
their mistake, but to this day, anyone I meet who comes from Yugoslavia marvels
at bananas and consider them a very special fruit.*

*My husband always remembered the great cry of joy that went out from everyone
on the ship when they first saw the Statue of Liberty.*

From Judith Turton of San Diego, California:

This recipe originated with my maternal grandmother, Latinka Stepanovich Milanovich, born in 1881 in Yugoslavia. She came to the U.S. in 1900. The recipe was passed down to my mother, Milka Milanovich Gantz, and my uncle, Samuel Gantz.

GRAS Y ZELA (SAUERKRAUT AND BEANS)

slices of fried pork chops, broiled wieners
 or pieces of cooked beef
1-2 onions, chopped
cloves of garlic, several
celery
1 can kidney beans
1 can sauerkraut
1 oz. vegetable oil
1 large tbsp. all-purpose flour
1 pint water

Cook onion, garlic and celery in frying pan, until tender. Put water in a pot and boil. Add beans and the onion, garlic and celery mixture. Add meat and let simmer. Be sure to stir to avoid scorching. Now add sauerkraut (after rinsing if the taste is too strong). Let simmer. In a large frying pan put oil and heat until it is very hot. Add one large tbsp. flour and keep stirring until mixture is very brown. You may have to do this for some time. Take several ladles of your beans and sauerkraut and put into the flour mixture. Stir and return to pot. Let set for a while before eating.

From Madeline Matson of Jefferson City, Missouri:

This is my grandmother's "Povatica" recipe, a Croatian nut-filled yeast bread. I grew up in the Croatian community of Strawberry Hill in Kansas City, Kansas. This community is still intact and has been written about by many sociologists and cultural historians.

I've tasted many different versions of Povatica. Some are made with honey and tend to be heavy; others are too doughy. My grandmother's version is, to me, the perfect balance of dough and filling. Made properly (with dough stretched thin), it is delectable. My mother put together the recipe while watching my grandmother make the bread, as she cooked without recipes.

I've traveled in Yugoslavia and seen a similar version of this bread in Slovenia. It was called "Potica."

My grandparent came to Kansas City, Kansas, from a village in Croatia in the early part of the twentieth century. Grandma made this rich, rolled nut bread for holidays and other special days. She was a master at stretching the dough thin. For weddings, women in the Croatian community of Strawberry Hill gathered together and made many loaves of Povatica for the two-day celebration.

POVATICA

Dough

All ingredients should be at room temperature.

2 cups lukewarm milk
1/2 cup sugar
2 tsp. salt
2 cakes compressed yeast (1/4 oz. each)
2 eggs, slightly beaten
1/2 cup soft butter
7 - 7 1/2 cups all-purpose flour

Mix together milk, sugar and salt. Crumble into yeast. Add eggs, and then add butter. Stir in sifted flour, adding a little at a time. After all ingredients are mixed, knead a little. Let rest until dough doubles in bulk. Depending on room temperature, this may take 1 to 2 hours. When doubled, cut into the number of loaves you want. (This recipe makes 3-4 loaf-size breads.) Knead each loaf until silky smooth. Let rise again until doubled. Then spread out each loaf with rolling pin and stretch across table as thin as possible. Spread with filling.

Filling

4 1/2 cups ground walnuts
3/4 cup scalded milk
1 1/2 cups sugar
3 eggs, slightly beaten
1 1/2 sticks butter (12 tbsp.)
1 1/2 tsp. salt
1 1/2 tsp. vanilla
3/4 tsp. ground lemon or orange rind
3 tbsp. cocoa

Mix ingredients well and spread on dough. Roll up dough into snake shape. Fit into loaf pan or angel cake pan. Brush tops with melted butter or beaten egg and sprinkle with sugar. Bake at 350° - 1 hour for angel cake pan and 45 minutes to 1 hour for loaf pans.

BELGIUM
FRANCE
HOLLAND
ITALY
PORTUGAL
SPAIN
SWITZERLAND

From Dolores Bultinck of Moline, Illinois:

My mother, Martha Bultinck-Clybouw, was born in Waardamme, West Flanders, Belgium. She came to America through Ellis Island in 1926. She brought these recipes with her.

BELGIAN BEEF BOUILLON WITH POTATOES

2-3 lbs. pot roast (soup meat or short ribs)
potatoes
salt
parsley

Boil beef in 2 quarts of water, slowly, until well done (about 2 hours). Remove meat. Measure out 2 to 3 cups of beef bouillon. Use the remainder for soup.

Cook potatoes in the 2-3 cups of bouillon. Add salt and parsley. When potatoes are done, drain and save bouillon. Mash potatoes and then add bouillon. Serve the beef with the potatoes.

HUTSEPOT (BOILED DINNER)

2 lbs. pork loin
1 cup leek
2 cups celery
1 onion
salt & pepper

3 1/2 lbs. potatoes
1 cup carrots
2 cups turnips
1 small savoy cabbage
2 quarts water

Brown meat thoroughly. Drain off fat, and add water. Clean vegetables and cut into small chunks. Add to the water. Bring to boil. Lower heat and simmer for 1 hour. Serves 8-10.

From Violet Dolson of Stonington, Connecticut:

My grandfather, Henri De Poortere (from Belgium), entered America through Ellis Island in September 1907. His departure was from the port of Liverpool, England, on the twenty-fifth of September.

This recipe was called "Birthday Cake" in my family, as it was the traditional cake baked for family members by my mother, who came from Belgium a year or so after her father.

BISCUIT DE REIMS

Take 9 eggs, weigh them and take same weight in sugar.
Take 6 eggs, weigh them and take same weight in flour.
Take 3 eggs, weigh them and take same weight in butter.

Beat the whites of 9 eggs till stiff. Fold in sugar. Then add the 9 egg yolks, well-beaten. Pour in flour gradually. Put in melted butter. Start baking in a slow oven - increase to moderate. It takes at least 1 hour to bake. A delicious cake!

From Donald and Rachelle Schopp of Bradenton, Florida:

In 1910, my father, Charles L. DePauw, came to the U.S. from Wateruliet, Belgium. After arriving at Ellis Island he took a train to Moline, Illinois, where many Belgian immigrants had settled to work for the thriving John Deere Plow and Planter Works. By 1920, Charles had worked hard, saved his money and paid cash for a small home. One thing was lacking: a wife. He had not found a woman who suited him and thinking back to a girl he had dated a few times in Belgium, he wrote to her and asked if she would care to come to the U.S. to be his wife. Here the story takes a strange twist. The return letter he received was not from the girl he had known but was instead from her younger sister, Amelie. She explained that the intended sister had married in the intervening years, but she herself was not married, was thirty years old, and was working as head cook in the home of a wealthy Belgian doctor. Since she had not found a spouse herself, she decided a life in the U.S. with a good man might be the best thing for both of them. She added that she would like to cook for her own husband and children in her own home rather than in a home where she was only an employee. They agreed to try it. Amelie arrived and they were married in 1920. It was a happy marriage and was blessed with two children, Frank, 1922, and Rachelle, 1926.

Somehow I feel their strange journey through Ellis Island was preordained so that my brother and I could be born in this wonderful country.

Belgian immigrants had this dish in their homes very often as they were very thrifty and loved cabbage.

ETSAPUT (ALL IN THE POT)

1 ham bone	6 cups ham, diced
1 stalk celery	2 or 3 medium size onions
2 bunches carrots	8 medium-size potatoes
1 large head cabbage	

Place bone and ham in large kettle. Cover with water. Add chopped onions and diced celery. Simmer for several hours. Add sliced carrots, diced potatoes and chopped cabbage to broth. Cook 1 hour. Remove ham bone. Let simmer until vegetables are tender. Long cooking time will improve flavor.

So simple, but so filling and good! One of the special things I can remember of my mother is the smell of this cooking in her kitchen.

From Yvonne Delaney Prestwich of Enfield, Connecticut:

Here is my grandmother's recipe for French Peas. Her name was Marie Louise Boyron.

She came over here with my grandfather, Gaston Boyron, my mother, Suzanne Josette, and my Aunt Irene from Marseilles, France. They came here when my mother was about nine, in 1922.

FRENCH PEAS

6 strips bacon
1 medium onion
1 15 oz. can young spring peas, drained or
 2 cups fresh, shelled peas
parsley flakes

In a cast-iron frying pan, fry bacon until medium cooked (not crisp). Remove bacon and set aside to drain. Cut in small pieces. Chop 1 onion and saute, until soft, in bacon drippings. Spoon off excess drippings. Add drained peas, bacon pieces, and some parsley flakes to frying pan. Mix and let heat up for about 8-10 minutes until peas are ready to serve. Serves 4 as a side vegetable.

From Bonnie Hauser of Iowa City, Iowa:

In the spring of 1986, at the age of eighty-two, in a red house on the corner in Adrian, Minnesota, Tena (Trientje DeLange) Broesder sat down and wrote her life experiences, being born in the Netherlands, November 20, 1903, and at the age of eight, migrating to the United States with her parents and four sisters. Two brothers were already living near Adrian. In Holland, the garden was their pride and joy, so lots of vegetables were raised and used. Potatoes were a must as they were used for everything that was stored in crocks and brine, for soups, plain cooked, fried and eaten three times a day. A big kettle was used for cooking, and it simmered all day with layers of raw potatoes, sliced carrots, turnips, onions, white dried beans that were soaked overnight, home-raised pork or ham, salt, and more of the same until the kettle was full. The water that was used to cook potatoes in was saved from the day before when the potatoes were cooked and served whole for Sunday dinner. Potato water was never discarded. To this day Mother still saves it and uses it for gravies, soups, and so forth. After this mixture was cooked, the meat was taken out and was put into a big cast-iron pan, browned and then served. Brei (buttermilk), thickened with pearl barley and simmered all day, was our dessert. All breads were bought at the bakery as there were no ovens in the stoves in Holland.

Mother's book called "Coming to America C.O.D." had been donated to the Ellis Island artifacts and also to a museum in Nieuweschens, Holland. My father was also from Holland and came to this country as a young man with his parents. His name was Casper Broesder.

BARLEY BREI (BRY)

Precook 1/2 cup of pearl barley until nearly done.

2 quarts milk
dash of salt
barley

Have 2 quarts milk heated to a boil, dash of salt and barley. Simmer on a very low fire. (Can use buttermilk in place of milk.)

COOKED CABBAGE (BOSCOOL)

1 layer raw sliced potatoes
1 head shredded cabbage

Put this together in layers. Several potatoes are used.

1/4 cup lard or oleo
dash of salt & pepper
1 cup milk
dash of nutmeg

Cook over a very low fire. When done, stir from bottom up.

OLE KOOKEN

These were made on New Year's Day and were the main meal.

1 quart liquid (milk or water)
(This is where the potato water was used.
 Liquid must be warm.)
2 pkgs. yeast
2 1/2 cups sugar
dash of salt
1/2 pkg. currants
8-10 cups all-purpose flour

Dissolve yeast in 2 cups of warm liquid. Leave to set 5 minutes. Add 1/2 cup of sugar and 2 cups of flour, mix so it looks like a spongy mixture. Add rest of water, sugar, salt, currants, and about 8 cups of flour. Set in a warm place for 2 to 3 hours, so it raises double or more in size. Heat 2 quarts of oil to 365°. Drop by tablespoon of dough into hot oil until brown. Sometimes they will turn themselves over. If not, turn over when one side is nice and brown. We love to drop them into the hot oil, so that they would have long tails on them. Roll into sugar and eat hot.

From Diana Sterett of Alamo, California:

I remember our boat trip and waiting each day to see the Statue of Liberty.

DUTCH COOKIES OR CAKE

2 cups self-rising flour
1 cup butter (2 sticks)
1 cup sugar
1 small egg
5 drops vanilla extract

For cookies, knead into smooth ball. Shape into 40 small balls 3/4" in diameter. Place and <u>press</u> on buttered baking sheet and bake in 350° preheated oven for 12-15 minutes or until golden brown.

For cake, after kneading into ball spread in cake pan and cook 350° for 30-35 minutes.

From Mrs. Charles R. Walgreen, III of Lake Forest, Illinois:

In 1911, Vincenzo and Francesca Bonsignore from Caltanissetta, Sicily, were among those heading toward a new life and future in the land of opportunity, America. After being processed through Ellis Island they made their way to Rochester, in Monroe County, New York. It was in Rochester that they opened Bonsignores Grocery Store. Mr. and Mrs. Bonsignore became the parents of my father, Albert, Calegere, Luigi and Mary, who helped their father in the store. On August 31, 1926, Vincenzo and Francesca achieved their dream of becoming American citizens when they received their "Certificate of Naturalization" from the United States Department Of Labor.

Bonsignores Grocery Store became known locally for its wonderful Italian Sausage (quite an honor in a city with a fairly large number of citizens with Italian heritage). While Bonsignores is no longer there, the sausage is still being made by the Bonsignores with strict adherence to their family recipe.

BONSIGNORES ITALIAN SAUSAGE

50 lbs. double-ground pork
 shoulder
6 cups grated parmesan cheese
6 tbsp. bottled Italian spices
6 tbsp. parsley
9 tbsp. freshly ground pepper
12 tbsp. salt

4 cups water
3 tbsp. ground sage
2 tbsp. crushed pepper
3 tbsp. dry mustard
3 tbsp. basil
10 tbsp. anise

Natural sausage casing

Mix all ingredients (except sausage casing) together. Push mixture through sausage machine into sausage casings, or make into patties.

This recipe makes 50 lbs. of sausage which may be frozen in zip-lock freezer bags for no longer than 6 months.

You may divide the recipe in half to make a smaller amount.

From George A. Alfano of Newburgh, New York:

Charles and Angelina Chuff-Alfano came over separately from Italy, met and married in New York City, and went to McKees Rocks, Pennsylvania, where they had many children. The Alfanos purchased a farm in Hudson Valley, New York. As most immigrants, Charles and Angelina were hard workers, and they struggled to keep a roof over the children's heads and food on the table. Charles was a laborer, stone crusher, and farmer. The children worked together picking beans and berries, selling tomatoes, and did whatever jobs provided them with a few pennies to add to the household. Angelina cleaned chickens for a nickel each. And of course, the family grew grapes to make the wine for the table.

WAND

2 lbs. all-purpose flour
2 1/2 tsp. salt
2 tsp. baking powder
13 eggs
black pepper (coarse), to taste

Make ring with flour - beat eggs, add salt, baking powder, and black pepper to flour. Put in beaten eggs (a little) at a time until all is absorbed by the flour. Keep rolling 10-15 minutes. Let flour (dough) ball sit for 10 minutes. Cut dough into 5-6 pieces and then roll to make small flat ball. Let sit 5-7 minutes. Roll out and cut into strips. Fold to make a bow and pinch ends tightly. Heat oil in pan and fry the strips as space allows, adding just enough oil to prevent from burning. Makes batch for 4-6 people.

Wand is a light, flaky, "spicy" "cookie" that Italians make around the holidays: Lent, Easter, Christmas. May be dunked in coffee, tea, or consumed alone for snacks. Can also be sprinkled with confectioners' sugar if desired.

From Theresa Scinto of Winter Springs, Florida:

My parents came through in 1929 from Castelfranco, Benevento, Italy, and also my husband's grandparents earlier, also from the same town. Castelfranco is a village in the province of Benevento. It is located in the mountains outside of Naples. In the 1800's living conditions were depressed. Day-to-day living was a struggle.

The news of America as a land of opportunity came to Castelfranco. Some young men took the trip to America to see if it was true. Their letters brought whole families to the United States. The Castels had two ideas in mind. Their first thought was to educate their children to have a better life than they had. Secondly, to secure this life, they must own property. They were willing to work hard to gain these ends. The railroads were hiring when the Castels got to America, so many of them worked on the New Haven railroad. This is how they settled in Connecticut.

Peddlers brought around the fruit and vegetables that they ate daily. Not only were they used to eating vegetables but in the new land, they were cheap as compared to meat. Some Castels started truck farming. As Connecticut developed and became a manufacturing area, the Castels worked in the factories. They bought their own homes as soon as they could. They were proud of their gardens and vegetables remained a staple in their diet.

Lorenzo, my husband's grandfather, was one of seven brothers who left Castelfranco for lands where a future could be built. He was one of the first Castels to come through Ellis Island to settle in the United States. This was in the 1880's.

His first job was with a steamship line. He helped many illiterate but hardworking immigrants fill out their papers and become citizens.

Through the years, Lorenzo had many business enterprises. The one that is remembered is the saloon on Hester Street in New York. The cost of an 8 oz. glass of beer was three cents and then it went up to five cents. There was wine, too. Along one wall of the saloon was a long mahogany bar. On the bar was all kinds of food that you could eat if you bought a beer.

There were pickled peppers, pickled tripe, tripe with tomato sauce and hot pepper, dried olives, lung and heart with hot pepper, snails with tomato sauce, provolone cheese, hard boiled eggs, and another big cheese called "casacaval" (translated it means "horse cheese"). There was also plenty of Italian bread made plain with flour, yeast, salt, and water.

Lorenzo knew what it was like to be hungry in a strange land, so at night any left over food went to an immigrant family with hungry children.

MARY SCINTO'S ITALIAN TOMATO SAUCE

1 16 oz. can Italian tomatoes
1 16 oz. can tomato sauce
1 tsp. sugar
salt & pepper, to taste
1/2 cup grated cheese
1 lb. macaroni, spaghetti or homemade noodles

Mash the tomatoes well and let simmer in a large saucepan or kettle for 1/2 hour. Stir occasionally.

While tomatoes are cooking, fry meat. Use meatballs, Italian sausage, beef brociola, lamb fore, or pork butt. Two or three of these meats in the sauce give a hearty flavor. Recipes follow.

Add tomato sauce to tomatoes. Rinse can with 1/2 cup water and add to tomatoes. Also add sugar, salt and pepper. Mix well.

Add meats and simmer 30-40 minutes, stirring occasionally. Sauce will thicken without a cover. Made a day or so ahead, kept in the refrigerator and then reheated slowly, the sauce will be tastier.

Cook macaroni according to directions on the package. Drain and put macaroni in a large dish or platter. Sprinkle 1/4 cup grated cheese over it, and pour 2 ladles of sauce on top. (1 ladle=1/4 cup) Turn macaroni gently to mix. Sprinkle the rest of the cheese on top and spread 3 ladles of sauce over all. Do not mix again before serving. Meat is served on an individual platter and extra sauce is served in a gravy boat. Use a large spoon and a fork to take out of the platter. Serves 4-6.

MEATBALLS

1 lb. ground chuck
2 slices stale bread, crumbled
1/2 tsp. parsley flakes
1 tbsp. raisins
1 clove garlic, grated

2 tbsp. Italian grated cheese
1/2 cup cold water
2 eggs
salt & pepper
1/4 cup oil or lard

Into a mixing bowl put ground chuck, bread, parsley flakes, raisins, garlic, grated cheese, salt and pepper. Mix well. Add cold water and mix. Add 2 eggs and mix. Form meatballs the size of a large egg. Wet your hands before making each meatball and the mixture will not stick to your hands. Put 1/4 cup oil in a large skillet and fry meatballs until brown on all sides. Makes 8-10 meatballs.

ITALIAN SAUSAGE

1 lb. Italian sausage, sweet or hot

Cut into serving pieces and fry slowly in large skillet until sausage is brown on all sides. Make sure the sausage is thoroughly cooked. Put into the tomato sauce and simmer 1/2 hour.

STEWED TRIPE

2 lbs. tripe
1/4 cup oil
1 clove garlic
1 large can tomatoes, mashed
1/2 tsp. oregano
1/2 tsp. hot pepper
salt
1 medium potato, cooked and diced (optional)

Get tripe that is already cleaned. Wash and put into a kettle or large saucepan. Cover with water and boil 1/2 hour. Drain and cool. When cool, cut into bite-size pieces. Put the oil in a large skillet. Add garlic, brown and remove. Add tomatoes and simmer 1/2 hour, stirring often. Add oregano, hot pepper, salt. Mix. Add tripe and potato if desired. Simmer altogether until tripe is tender, about 1/2 hour. Test the tripe with a fork. Serve over boiled rice or cooked linguini macaroni. Serves 4-6.

From Josephine Orlando Saiia of Greenfield, Wisconsin:

This recipe sustained many immigrants on their voyage to Ellis Island and their new homes. Travelers would order suitcases full of these cookies to eat on board as the dining rooms were too expensive. They are very, very hard when dry and become chewy when damp -- like an ocean voyage. They do not spoil, can be eaten for a year, keep well with no crumbs. Pack well. I have one that's fifty years old. These are made by special bakers and were often made in fancy shapes -- animals, flowers, baskets, etc., and sold as gifts at festivals.

We come from Cosenza, Italy. My grandfather came through Ellis Island with these cookies many times between late 1890's and World War I. My father came in 1906, made many trips. Then served in the U.S. Army in WWI and became a citizen, so when my mother and I came in March 1926, -- we did not go through Ellis Island because we were listed as "returning to U.S.A.". Because we were citizens, we were taken off the ship before it docked at Ellis Island.

MUSTASOLE (HARD COOKIE)

3 cups sifted all-purpose flour (in bowl)
1 1/2 cups sifted all-purpose flour (in cup)
1 1/2 cups melted honey, warm
1/4 tsp. salt
1/2 tsp. vanilla
  or lemon flavor

Place 3 cups flour in bowl, add hot honey, salt, flavor and mix well. Add more flour to make very stiff dough, knead on a board till smooth. Place in bowl and cover and let rest for at least 12 hours, not in refrigerator. Divide in 4 pieces - knead each till smooth, using little flour. Shape as you would children's clay - build on ungreased cookie sheets - add little oil on top and shine, or water to make it stick. Bake at 325° for 15 to 20 minutes (gas or electric varies) till golden brown. Remove from pan while hot and lay on flat surface to harden. (Limp when hot - hard when cold.) No crumbs.

From Leida DiScipio Schunk of Williamsville, New York:

There are many of these recipes that never make the cookbooks. My children remember my father coming home with shopping bags full of dandelions and other weeds that he picked along the roadways and fields. It had become a way of life for him. They accepted it as something Grandpa liked - their friends thought it was strange. Today, these weeds are appearing on menus in the best of places. My mother and I left Naples, Italy, on the ninth of December, 1937, aboard the Saturnia and arrived in New York on December 20, 1937. I have my passport and immigration identification card and a few other old pictures. I was eight years old.

POTATOES & DANDELIONS

4 to 6 potatoes
2 quart basket or more dandelions
Free. If fresh picked, best before they flower. Clean & wash thoroughly.
1/4 cup olive oil
2 or 3 cloves garlic, chopped
1/2 tsp. red pepper (hot), crushed

Boil potatoes in large pan about half an hour; depending on size, add dandelions and continue cooking till both are tender. Remove from water (water makes excellent base for soups), peel & mash potatoes, cut dandelions if large, and mix together. In large skillet, saute garlic and red pepper in olive oil about a minute. Add potatoes and dandelions and continue to cook another 15 minutes. Enjoy with fresh crusty Italian bread and dry red wine.

You may also use leftover mashed potatoes.

From Jeanette Caruso of Bloomington, Illinois:

My folks came from Continsa, Italy, and both came to Ellis Island. They both came over on the same boat but did not know each other. They later met and got married, then moved to Bloomington, Illinois.

STUFFED ARTICHOKES

8-12 artichokes
2 lbs. Italian bread crumbs
1 1/2 cups grated romano cheese
1 1/2 cups chopped parsley
10 cloves garlic, cut up

1/2 tsp. salt
1 tsp. pepper
1 oz. lemon juice
olive oil

Cut tops off a little and soak in lemon juice, then put upside down. Pull apart and stuff with mixed ingredients. Cook in pan with small amount of water and steam, then drain and put your oil on them.

M.S. SATURNIA

From Cynthia Abate-Upson of South Lawrence, Massachusetts:

"When are we going to make the baskets?" my cousins and I would ask every year around Eastertime. Our moms would smile as they remembered asking the same question, at the same time of year, and about at the same ages of their own mom. My grandmother, Santa Petroccione, even as a child, would ask the question to her mother; the only difference was she'd ask in Italian, her first language.

As I understand it, this same tradition occurred in many Italian families both here after immigration and before "in the old country." In fact, I recall a few years ago being in Boston's North End in an Italian Bakery about four days before Easter. While waiting in line, I was surprised how many people (especially the older customers) would nod and smile as they glimpsed at the trays of baskets awaiting sale on the counter. Many commented on them as they recalled their past Easters.

These baskets remind people of Italian descent of home, family, and childhood. The anticipation of coloring eggs, molding and shaping dough, and giving as a perfect Easter gift to friends and neighbors one's handiwork was exciting to a child!

Now, even in the 1990's, my family and I keep the tradition going, using the same recipe brought over from Sicily, Italy, by my great-grandmother,(Nana) Dorothea Bonacorsi Bounanno, in 1922. I hope you share the joy at the Easter season for many years to come by making and giving these baskets as my family before me has.

Although I use food coloring instead of beet juice (as my grandmother did) or other vegetable dyes for the eggs, this Cookie-Basket recipe hasn't changed in many years! We grew up calling them "baskets," but they are also remembered for their Italian name "cudure con louve," literally, basket with egg (pronounced "ku-doo-rey coo-low").

ITALIAN EASTER-EGG BREAD BASKET

Color eggs first, set oven for 350°. Line 2 cookie sheets with foil -- makes 6 baskets.

6 cups all-purpose flour, sifted	1 cup corn oil
4 1/2 tsp. baking powder	1 1/2 tsp. vanilla
1 cup sugar	7 eggs
colored sprinkles	milk & egg white, for brushing

To color eggs (6), boil 1/2 cup water (for each desired color), add 1 tsp. vinegar. Add 10 drops of desired food color. Roll egg in water solution. Take pan off stove - let egg dry on spoon.

Combine sifted flour, baking powder and sugar. Set aside. Beat together, eggs, oil & vanilla. Knead with spoon, while adding dry mixture to egg mixture, a little at a time. Knead with hands on a clean surface until evenly mixed. Do not over knead. On foil-lined tin, shape a cupful of dough into a basket shape. Place colored egg in center and cover with a small piece of rolled dough sealing edges to basket. Using hands, roll a 1" wide, 6" long piece of dough lengthwise - then curve to resemble basket handles. Attach by pressing with fingers to basket. Brush basket with egg white and apply sprinkles. Then brush with milk.

Bake 20 minutes at 350° on foil-lined cookie sheet. Let cool before removing with wide spatula. Serve or give on paper plates with decorated border. Wrap in plastic, tie with colored ribbon for a traditional and unique Easter cookie gift ! Makes 6 baskets.

From Gloria Montani Lear of North Walpole, New Hampshire:

My mother and her family arrived at Ellis Island from northern Italy in 1892. She was just about six years old. Her relatives were in the hotel business in New York, and she grew up in the wonderful era of the 1890's. She taught us (five daughters) the wonderful popular songs of the time, as well as instilling in us a love of opera music, since her sister and brother-in-law were associated in public relations for the Metropolitan Opera Company. The family hobnobbed with Gigli, Caruso, Melba, etc., and we loved hearing stories about them.

When our situation got lean in the late 1920's, Mom had to make do with very basic foods. One recipe, which follows, was served hunter-style, with polenta, a fine-grained cornmeal mush. It really stuck to the ribs on a cold winter evening!

STEWED BEEF KIDNEYS ITALIENNE

beef kidney
salt & pepper
onion
2 cloves garlic
oil

parsley
tomato paste
2 bay leaves
mushrooms, optional

Split a beef kidney, salt generously and let stand overnight. Drain and cut into small pieces, removing fat, muscle, etc., and rinse in two or three waters. Place in warm frying pan and render over medium heat, stirring occasionally, until quite dry, draining as liquid gathers. Brown an onion and a couple of cloves of garlic in small amount of oil. Saute kidney and a sprinkling of parsley with onion for a short while (10-15 minutes) over a low heat. Add about 1 tsp. of tomato paste, salt, pepper, and a couple of bay leaves and simmer until tender. Mushrooms added to the sauce is optional.

From Norma Falce of The Bronx, New York:

My dad came from Italy in 1906 and worked as a laborer. He had to save enough money for passage for my mother and my brother, who was a small boy. After three years, he finally had put enough money together for his family to come. As many others, they came steerage, where they slept on the floor of the ship.

Christmas Eve, 1908, my mother and brother arrived at Ellis Island with no one to meet them. They had to wait till the next morning, when they were taken to Jersey City, with tags pinned to them and put on a train (not knowing where they were going), and rode for twelve hours. Finally the conductor took them off and my dad met them at Hornell, New York, a small village upstate where they lived out their lives for over sixty years.

The recipes that I am giving are really what we were able to afford. I remember very lean years, for a long time to come, so we named them Poor Man's recipes.

POOR MAN'S PIZZA

Everyone made their own bread. There were no bakeries in small towns, so my mother would take some bread dough and flatten it out on a cookie sheet or pizza pan and let it rise for half an hour. Again, then with her fingers, she would make indentations pressing her fingers down into the dough. She would brush it with olive oil and make sure it would go into the grooves, then sprinkle chopped garlic and oregano and bake for about 30 minutes at 400°.

POOR MAN'S LUNCH

Panne Cotto

Enough stale bread, as needed, broken up small. Put aside in a dish.

One large onion sauteed in 1/4 cup olive oil. When limp, add as much water as needed for the bread to soak. When the water and onion and oil have come to a good boil, break the eggs and poach them into the juice.

When your eggs are nicely coated and cooked to your taste, remove and pour over the stale bread till the bread is soaked and soft. Salt and pepper, to taste.

From Alyce Barone of Union City, California:

My grandparents arrived in America via Ellis Island, and I proudly submit a recipe from the Campagna region, from which they came. This is from my grandmother, M. Rafaela Barone.

PIZZA RUSTICA (COUNTRY HAM, SAUSAGE AND CHEESE PIE)

<u>Crust</u>

2 cups all-purpose flour
1 tsp. salt
1/2 tsp. sugar
2 eggs
1/4 cup oil
1/2 pkg. active dry yeast, dissolved
1/4 cup water

Put flour and sugar in warm bowl. Mix well. Add eggs, oil and dissolved yeast. Mix and form into ball. Place a little oil on dough and in bowl. Cover and let rise until double. Everything must be at room temperature. Roll crust as for a pie.

<u>Filling</u>

Grease deep pie pan, sprinkle with flour. Cut into small pieces and arrange in layers into bottom crust:

1/2 lb. cooked, cooled sausage, cut into small pieces
1/2 lb. ham, cut into small pieces
1/2 lb. monterey jack cheese, in small pieces
1/4 cup grated parmesan cheese
2 or 3 eggs, beaten

Repeat all layers until filling is used up. Pour beaten eggs over filling. Put top crust on pie. Cut slits in top crust, brush with beaten egg. Bake at 350° until slightly brown, then lower oven to 300° and bake 1 hour longer. Lower heat a little if pie cooks too fast. Traditionally served at Easter.

From Jack Scordo of Watertown, New York:

My mother, Mrs. Vincenzo (Marianna) Scordo, came through Ellis Island from Italy in 1916.

I am delighted to submit a recipe which my mother brought over from Italy. This is a dish which was prepared on the Feast of St. Joseph (March 19th) which is celebrated all over Italy and the United States.

RICOTTA CHEESE BALLS (MEATLESS MEATBALLS)

2 lbs. ricotta cheese
3 cups bread crumbs
2 tsp. parsley

1 tsp. cloves
1 cup romano cheese
1/2 dozen eggs

Mix all ingredients together. With hands, shape into balls, then flatten. Fry in deep fat slowly until brown on both sides. Then drain them on paper towels. Makes about 3 dozen.

This is a side dish with perciatelli macaroni and cooked spinach, which was a meatless dinner for St. Joseph's Feast Day.

From Ms. Margaret DeVito of Utica, New York:

MARGARET'S CRUNCHY BREADSTICKS

4 cups all-purpose flour
1/2 cup vegetable oil
2 pkgs. active, dry yeast (1/4 oz.
 each)
1/2 cup of warm water (or more if
 necessary)

2 1/4 tsp. fennel seeds
1/2 tsp. salt

Dissolve yeast in warm water. Add oil to mixture. When well mixed, blend in flour and salt. Knead for 10 minutes. Sprinkle in fennel seeds and continue kneading for another 10 minutes. Add a little more water if necessary to make a soft dough. Cover, let rise for 1 hour. After dough has risen, punch down. Roll dough into long ropes and cut into lengths desired. You can also form into round rings. They are called Tarreli. Bake in a 375° oven for about 25-30 minutes.

From Nancy Anne McClure Zeller of Albany New York:

My mother's father, Michele Borella, immigrated from Castellamonte, Piedmont, which is thirty miles north of Torino, through Ellis Island in 1905.

This recipe is for "meat relish," a traditional northern Italian recipe which we pronounced "bonya cowda," but which I have since learned is spelled "bagna calda," meaning "warm bath."

Mother would prepare a batch of this sauce in the morning before a holiday meal. It would simmer on the stove all morning and be available whenever anyone wanted it. It served as an appetizer before the big turkey dinner; I'm sure the liberal dose of garlic and olive oil helped prepare our systems internally for the overeating that was to follow. We would grab a big chunk of Italian bread and, using it to catch drips, we would dip celery, green peppers or cabbage into the pot of hot green sauce. When the bread was thoroughly soaked, we would eat that too. Oftentimes three or four relatives would be crowded around the stove, dipping from the pot.

This concoction of parsley and fresh spinach plus garlic is called a meat relish, but it could be a tasty hors d'oeuvre served on crackers. You can add a whisper of it to salads.

MEAT RELISH

1 bunch parsley
1 lb. fresh spinach
3 or 4 cloves garlic, according to taste
hot pepper, to taste
1/2 cup olive oil
1/4 cup vinegar
8 oz. flat fillet anchovies

Grind ingredients finely in food chopper.
Mix thoroughly. Heat on top of stove
in pot or flameproof casserole.

From Frances Van Orden of Corpus Christi, Texas:

My mother, Frances Martucci, was born in Montefusco, a province of Avallino, Italy. She was born to Caroline Lombardi Martucci and John Martucci. She had one brother, Fortunato. My grandfather, John, came to America two years before his family joined him. He was a barber and worked to save money for their voyage.

My mother told me about the long and anxious wait they had at Ellis Island in 1903, always worried they would be rejected. All went well and they moved to the Lower East Side in New York and eventually to the Bronx.

LA CREMA ITALIANA

4 yolks of eggs
1 whole egg
1 quart milk
2 tbsp. full of cornstarch
6 tbsp. full of sugar

Must pass through sieve twice before cooking with one skin of lemon. Be sure to turn always the same. Mix starch and sugar together.

COFFEE CAKE

Top Mixture	Cake
3 tbsp. flour	1/2 cup butter
1 tbsp. cinnamon	1 cup sugar
1 tbsp. sugar	2 eggs
3 tbsp. shortening	1 cup milk
	2 cups all-purpose flour
	4 tsp. baking powder

Make dough from cake ingredients. For topping, mix dry ingredients. Rub in shortening and spread thickly over top of dough before baking. Makes one 9" coffee cake. Bake at 350° for 45 minutes.

From Carmine Vicenzo of Middletown, Connecticut:

My parents came to Ellis in 1936 from a small Italian village called Sepino, Campobasso, located in the Molise region of Italy. The following is one treasured recipe from my mom's collection, which is a favorite during the winter holidays.

RAVIOLI DULCI (SWEET RAVIOLIS)

<u>Dough</u>

1 3/4 cups unbleached flour
2 tbsp. water
2 tbsp. dry white wine
1 tbsp. olive oil
2 egg yolks

Mix all together, forming a ball and place under a covered bowl for 1/2 hour, then roll out thin and using a round cutter cut out circular discs.

<u>Filling</u>

8 chestnuts, boiled and peeled
1/4 cup almonds
2 tbsp. honey
1 square melted, unsweetened chocolate
1 tbsp. each grated lemon rind and orange rind
2 tbsp. candied citron
1/2 tsp. each: nutmeg, cinnamon, vanilla

Mix thoroughly in food processor. Fill the center of the circular disc with a full teaspoon of filling mixture. Fold side to other side in a half-moon shape and press sides together to seal. Fry in very hot oil, drain on towels. After cooling sprinkle with confectioners' sugar. Enjoy with strong coffee, either demitasse or expresso.

From Carmelita Mundo Peters of Bluefield, West Virginia:

My father, Joseph Mundo, immigrated to the United States in 1905 with his mother and older sister. His father had been there for several years. My father, who was six at the time, told the story that when he and his sister Mary (who was eight) first glimpsed the Statute of Liberty, Mary accidentally poked my father in the eye. Because of a "red eye," my grandmother, father, and sister, Mary, were detained and not permitted to join my grandfather immediately. My father said that the accidental poking of his eye, combined with his comment, "Who's the man with the funny mustache?" (his father), caused a rocky relationship to develop between the two!

SPINACH PIE

Filling Ingredients

3 lbs. fresh spinach or swiss chard   6 cloves of garlic, chopped
1 tsp. salt   4-6 tbsp. olive oil
1 tsp. pepper

Wash, remove stems, and coarsely chop the spinach or swiss chard. Drain well. Place in large mixing bowl. Add the salt, pepper, and garlic. Add olive oil and toss until all the greens are coated and the seasonings are distributed. Set aside.

Pie Crust

Use your own favorite recipe (decrease amount of shortening by at least 1/3 cup) or use the following:

3 cups all-purpose flour   1 tsp. salt
2/3 cup vegetable shortening   6-8 tbsp. ice water

Cut the shortening into the flour until crumbly. Add ice water (start with 6 tbsp.) and mix. Add more water if necessary in order to make a dough which is not sticky. Roll into 9" circles (thin). Place heaping amounts of filling on half the dough. Heap filling high because filling will compress when cooked. Flip other half of dough over the filling and seal edges with a pie crust edging. This will appear to resemble a large tart. Bake at 400° until golden brown. Yield: 4-6 pies. (Depends upon thickness of crust and uniformity of circles).

Swiss chard and beet tops are far more flavorful than spinach. However, spinach is available all year round. Some people use bread dough. The flavor is different, but also very good. I can remember that summer was "special" because we raided the garden for the first beet tops and swiss chard in order to make these pies.

From Renato and Helen Pandolfi of Newark, Delaware:

My dad, Edgardo, came to the United States in 1919, traveling third class on an ocean liner. After that experience, he vowed when his wife Josephine followed, she would travel second class. He immediately went to work as a bus boy at the Waldorf-Astoria Hotel in New York City to save money for her trip.

POLLO DI FANO

2 small fryers, cut up in small pieces
(omit backs and use to make stock)
3 tbsp. butter
3 tbsp. oil
half of a medium onion
1 large clove of garlic, crushed
1 tsp. parsley

Sprig of fresh dill
or 1/2 tsp. dried dill
1/2 tsp. rosemary
(rubbed between fingers)
1 cup dry white wine
or can of beer
salt & pepper, to taste

In large skillet combine butter, oil, onion, garlic, parsley and herbs all together. Just as it begins to melt add chicken pieces. Cover and cook on medium heat. After a few minutes, turn all at once with spatula brushing bottom of skillet. Cover and continue cooking until lightly brown. Uncover. Keep cooking and turning until nicely browned and much of liquid evaporated. Add salt and pepper, wine or beer, cover and let it all blend together for a few minutes. Serve with green vegetable, risotto or plain rice.

RISOTTO

1 garlic clove, small
1/2 small onion
2 tbsp. butter
1 cup uncooked rice

2 cans or so of
College Inn Chicken Broth or
Chicken Stock
1 cup parmesan cheese
1 tbsp. butter

Saute onion until limp in 2 tbsp. butter. Add uncooked rice and stir. Add chicken broth gradually, in intervals, as needed, until rice is the consistency you like, and all liquid is evaporated. Add extra butter and cup of cheese.

If you enjoy rice as a first course, Mother added to one cup of rice 3/4 of a lb. of sweet Italian sausage out of the skin. She browned it with butter and onion and then added rice as above.

From Majorie Paci Ellingwood of Windsor, Connecticut:

Here is a recipe for Polenta which my Italian (Tuscany) immigrant father, John Paci, brought from Monte St. Savino. As a growing child, I must confess it was not one of my favorites, but now in my grandma years, we enjoy it, and even my Irish husband has learned how to stir, stir, stir. . . .

POLENTA

1 lb. cornmeal
1 1/2 - 2 quarts boiling water
2 tsp. salt
(optional: 1 1/2 lbs. cooked sausage meat)

Pour cornmeal slowly into boiling water, stir constantly with a wooden spoon (we had a "polenta paddle"). Cook for 30 minutes or until meal leaves sides of pot easily. My papa would now add chunks of cooked sausage meat.

Turn contents onto bread board to cool down. Papa would slice through the mound of cornmeal (horizontally) with a piece of string, and insert slices of melting cheese in each layer. Sprinkle top with romano/parmesan grated cheese, and spoon sauce over your individual slices. Yummm. The next two days (or so) we would slice pieces off the mold, and fry them till browned in olive oil.

From Filomena Commisso of West Babylon, New York:

My mom doesn't usually cook with measurements. She cooks with "a pinch of this and a pinch of that." She has given this recipe to her friends, but they still love hers the best. Mom came here from Calabria, Italy, in the 1950's.

FILOMENA'S STUFFED EGGPLANT

8 Italian eggplants
breadcrumbs, enough to mix with rest of mixture
2-3 cloves garlic, chopped
3-4 sprigs fresh parsley, chopped
5 leaves of fresh basil, chopped
3 eggs
1 lb. chopped meat
1/2 cup pecorino romano grated cheese
olive oil

Boil eggplant until cooked. Remove eggplants from water, drain, then peel. Set eggplant skins aside. In another bowl, mix pulp of eggplants together with all of the above ingredients. Take the eggplant skins and stuff with this mixture. Make sure olive oil is hot enough before frying the stuffed eggplants (or else they will stick to the pan). If there is any leftover mixture, make hamburger patties and fry in olive oil without their skins. After they are cooked, top with tomato sauce and sprinkle grated cheese on top. Serve hot.

From Elsie B. Silva of San Diego, California:

The following recipe was brought to this country from the Azores Islands, Portugal, in the early part of the 20th century by my grandmother, Maria Freitas.

FISH STEAKS IN PORTUGUESE SAUCE

1 tbsp. oil
2 onions
1/2 cup green pepper, all chopped
1/4 cup celery
2 tbsp. parsley
2 cloves garlic
4 halibut steaks
 or any white, firm-fleshed fish
1 (15 oz.) can tomato sauce
salt & pepper, to taste
bay leaf
1/2 tsp. cumin
1 (3") piece orange peel

Saute all vegetables in oil until golden. Add more oil if necessary. Add tomato sauce, 1/2 can (sauce can) of water, salt & pepper to taste, cumin, bay leaf and orange peel. Simmer 10 minutes. Poach fish steaks in sauce until fish flakes easily with a fork (about 10-15 minutes). While fish is cooking spoon sauce over steaks so top is cooked evenly. Discard orange peel & bay leaf.

Serve with boiled potatoes sprinkled with dill weed and butter, green salad, and a good crusty Italian or French bread.

From Mary I. Seevers of Fairfield, California:

My mother, Maria Paiva Rodrigues, came here from Paol du Mar, Madeira Islands, in 1910 with her son Manuel G. Rodrigues. My father arrived earlier to establish a home to receive them.

BEANS

1 lb. dried pink beans
2 links linguisa
2 tbsp. fat
1 or 2 lbs. hamburger,
 ham hocks, or bacon
1 onion
1/2 tsp. cumin

1/4 tsp. dry mustard
1/4 tsp. black pepper
1/4 tsp. allspice
2 small cans tomato sauce
1 or 2 cans water
salt

Soak beans overnight or 6 to 8 hours. No salt, please. Cover with at least 3" of water over the top of the beans. When ready to cook, cook in same water -- add more if dry. Add several slices of bacon or ham hocks. Bring to boil, simmer for 1 hour or more until the beans are soft but firm. Make sauce while beans cook. Cut 2 links of linguisa in 1" pieces, brown slowly turning over to brown all sides in 2 tbsp. fat. Remove from pan. Brown 1 or 2 lbs. hamburger until pink is gone. Add 1 diced onion, 1/2 tsp. cumin, 1/4 tsp. dry mustard, 1/4 tsp. black pepper, 1/4 tsp. allspice, 2 small cans tomato sauce, 1 or 2 cans water, salt. Simmer 10 minutes with the linguesa thrown in. Add to beans, simmer 10 minutes more. Serve with chopped onions, shredded cheese, and French bread.

From Ecilda de Azevedo Tracey of Forked River, New Jersey:

GIGACETA

1 small onion, chopped
2 cloves garlic, chopped
1/4 lb. linguise sausage, sliced
16 oz. can kidney beans

1/8 tsp. salt
dash pepper
1 1/2 cups water, boiling

Fry onion, garlic and sausage all together in olive oil for 5 minutes (low flame). Add rest of ingredients along with 1 cup white rice and cover. Cook all this together 30 to 45 minutes.

From Sue Svrcek of Donora, Pennsylvania:

My mother, Hope Perez Ibanez, came to America (Ellis Island) when she was fourteen (1916). She came with an older brother (they were orphans). She had to return to Spain because her brother had smallpox. She returned to America when she was sixteen with her husband. Her brothers didn't know what to do with her and were too poor themselves to feed her, so they married her off. She came from a family of twelve: ten brothers, one sister.

GYPSY'S ARM (BRAZO GITANO)

8 eggs, room temperature
8 tbsp. sugar
8 tbsp. all-purpose flour, divided
1/2 egg shell of milk
1/2 tsp. vanilla

Separate eggs. Beat egg whites until stiff but not dry. Set aside. Beat sugar and egg yolks until creamy. Add half the flour and the milk. Beat well and add the rest of the flour. Gently fold in the egg whites and vanilla. Grease a large jelly roll pan. Spread the mixture evenly on the pan. Bake at 350° for 20 to 25 minutes. While cake is still warm, loosen it from the pan and invert on a dampened tea towel. Roll it up and set aside until you are ready to fill with custard filling. When filled, refrigerate for at least an hour before cutting into serving slices. Makes 12 servings.

Custard Filling

1/3 cup sugar	2 egg yolks
3 tbsp. cornstarch	2 cups scalded milk
1/4 tsp. salt	1 tsp. vanilla

Combine sugar, cornstarch, salt and egg yolks. Beat thoroughly. Add enough scalded milk to make a smooth paste. Add paste to remaining milk. Place mixture in the top of the double boiler with the water boiling. Stir constantly until mixture is thick. Cool. Add vanilla. Preparation time: cake - 40 minutes, filling - 30 minutes.

This filling may be made a few days before using in Gypsy's Arm, cream puffs etc. Must be refrigerated. Moderately difficult.

Chicken with rice is made all over Spain and each province makes it differently.

CHICKEN WITH RICE/PAELLA/ARROZ CON POLLO

1 1/2 chicken fryers (3 lbs.), cut up
1 lb. lean pork, cubed
1/2 cup olive oil
1 medium onion, chopped
2 fresh cloves, minced (or more)
1 large tomato, peeled, seeded & chopped
1 sprig parsley

2 cups uncooked rice (River brand)
1 tsp. lemon juice
1 bay leaf
1 tsp. salt *
pinch of toasted saffron
1 cup hot chicken broth
1/4 cup dry white wine
2 1/4 cups chicken broth

Heat the oil and saute the chicken until golden and place in large casserole. Do same to pork. Strain the drippings and saute the pepper and onion in the drippings until transparent. Add tomato, garlic, lemon juice, bay leaf, and salt.* Mix well and cook until mushy. Set skillet aside. Heat the 1 cup of broth and dissolve the crushed saffron in the broth. Add wine to the broth and pour this mixture into the skillet. Add the parsley and mix well. Pour this mixture into the chicken and pork. Cover and cook over medium heat until the chicken is tender, about 15 minutes. Add the 2 1/4 cups of broth and the rice. STIR CAREFUL ONCE!! Bring to a boil. Cover and place in a preheated 325° oven for 20 minutes only. Remove - let stand 15 minutes covered. Remove lid.

To toast saffron: Cut a square (3" x 3") of brown paper and place a few strands of saffron in center. Fold until the saffron is hidden, place on the lid of a boiling pot for about 20 minutes. Remove and crush while in paper.

* If using canned broth, use less salt.

From Morris Varon of Montgomery, Alabama:

My mother and father were Sephardic Jews, who came to America in 1912.

PESCADO CON HUEVO AND LEMON
(FISH WITH LEMON AND EGG SAUCE)

1 lb. fish filet
1 cup water
1 tsp. salt
dash pepper

2 tbsp. olive oil
juice of 2 lemons
2 eggs
fresh parsley

Place fish in shallow pan. Add water, pepper, salt & oil. Cook in oven under medium heat for 10-12 minutes. Turn heat off. Beat eggs with lemon juice then add some hot juice from fish. Stir constantly until well mixed. Pour sauce over fish -- add parsley. Serve hot or cold.

QUASADO DE CARNE AND SPINACH

6 matzos soaked in milk
 (most of milk squeezed out)
1 1/2 lbs. ground beef
1 tbsp. Spanish olive oil
2 tsp. salt

pepper, to taste
1 lb. fresh spinach
10 eggs, beaten
1/2 cup chicken broth

Brown meat in oil. Add salt & pepper. Add matzos, spinach & chicken stock to cool meat mixture and mix well. Add eggs last. Bake in greased, heated 9" x 13" pan at 375° for 1/2 hour.

From Ida M. Coleman of Whitesboro, New York:

My parents, along with some other relatives, came from Switzerland and passed through Ellis Island in 1910. I'm sharing a recipe that my mother (Alice Miller Minnig) brought from Switzerland. She always made this bread during the Christmas season and I'm carrying on that tradition.

ZUPFA (BRAIDED SWISS EGG BREAD)

2 pkgs. dry yeast (1/4 oz. each)
1 cup warm water
1 tbsp. sugar
1/2 cup all-purpose flour

Make a sponge of this group of ingredients - let rise until light about 20 minutes in warm place but not too hot.

1 cup milk	1/2 cup sugar
6 oz. butter	3 eggs, beaten
1 1/2 lbs. all-purpose flour	2 tsp. salt

Scald milk, add butter. Let cool. Add to the sponge 1 1/2 lbs. flour, milk and butter, 1/2 cup sugar, eggs, salt. Knead until smooth -- you can tell there's enough flour when dough can be worked and no longer sticks to the hands. Let rise until double in bulk. Make into braids (1 or 2 loaves) let it rise again. Just before baking, brush top of braids with beaten egg. Bake at 350°, 25 to 30 minutes.

From Judy Holderbach of Stillwater, Minnesota:

My grandparents, John and Martha Friedli, arrived at Ellis Island from Switzerland in the early 1920's. My grandma often recalled how young women with pretty hair had their hair shaved off. She said it was used to make wigs. They settled in Wisconsin where my grandfather was a cheesemaker. They returned to Switzerland in 1927 but came back to the U.S. in 1928. The trips across the ocean were long and hard on people.

They returned to Wisconsin, where my grandfather owned and operated several cheese factories. In 1946, they moved their family to Aldrich, Minnesota, where they owned and operated a cheese factory, cheese store, and cafe for more than thirty years. My grandmother was a wonderful and interesting person. She told many stories about her past and her years in Switzerland. She was also a very good cook.

BUTTERSCOTCH CANDY

1 cup white sugar
1 cup brown sugar
1/4 cup light corn syrup

1 cup water
1/3 cup butter
1 tsp. vanilla

Put sugars, syrup, and water in pan. Cook and stir until sugar is dissolved then cook without stirring to the stiff ball stage - 250°. Add butter and cook to medium-crack stage (280°) or brittle stage (300°). Remove from heat, add flavoring and pour in greased pan. Mark while still warm and when cool, break into pieces.

SWISS CAKE

10 egg yolks
1 cup sugar
lemon rind

Beat sugar & egg yolks until white in color. Put in lemon rind.

10 egg whites
1 cup all-purpose flour

Beat egg whites stiff and carefully mix in flour.

Blend alternately two mixtures. Put in layer pans. Cook at 375° for 35 minutes. Cool. Cut layers in half, so you end up with 4 layers. Fill layers with following:

Filling

6 eggs
3/4 cup sugar
vanilla
4 tsp. melted chocolate
1/2 lb. whipped butter

Cook in double boiler until thick. Let cool. Add 4 tsp. of melted chocolate and 1/2 lb. whipped butter.

From Leonore Chaplik of Sun City West, Arizona:

This is from a collection of my mother, Bertha Schedler, who came through Ellis Island from Switzerland in 1921.

SALZBURGER NOCKERL

3 tbsp. butter
5 eggs, separated, to room temperature
pinch of salt
3 tsp. sugar
1/3 cup confectioners' sugar
1/3 cup all-purpose flour
2 tbsp. cream sherry

In shallow round 10" baking dish or skillet, melt butter while preheating oven to 350°. In medium bowl, beat egg whites with salt just until they hold a peak. Sprinkle with 2 tsp. sugar, best until whites are stiff but not dry. In large bowl, beat egg yolks with confectioners' sugar about 1 minute. With rubber spatula, stir in flour and sherry. Stir about 1/4 of egg whites into egg yolks mixture, then fold in remaining whites (do not overfold). Tilt baking dish to coat bottom with melted butter. Spoon 6 mounds egg mixture into baking dish. Bake 10-12 minutes. Sprinkle with remaining sugar. Serve at once. Makes 6 servings.

From Mrs. Robert Patey of Springfield, Illinois:

This is my "secret" recipe for cookies, which has been handed down from generation to generation, beginning with Mrs. Johann Steiner in Switzerland.

Baking ammonia or ammonium carbonate used to be readily available in drug stores by the common name of HARTSHORN. Now I must send for it from the Maid of Scandinavia Co. at 3244 Raleigh Avenue South, Minneapolis, Minnesota 55416.

Christmas wouldn't be Christmas without these cookies brought from the "Old World."

GRANDMA STEINER'S CHRISTMAS COOKIES

2 cups sugar
2 cups butter
2 cups sweet milk
4 eggs

1 ounce baking ammonia
7 cups all-purpose flour
1/2 tsp. salt

Dissolve baking ammonia crystals in the milk. Cream butter and sugar. Beat in eggs, add flour and milk alternately. Add salt. Roll out dough on floured board. Cut with Christmas cutters. Bake 8-10 minutes at 350°.

ICING FOR GRANDMA STEINER'S CHRISTMAS COOKIES

1 1/2 cups sugar
1/3 cup water
2 eggs whites
1/4 tsp. anise oil

Boil sugar and water until is spins a thread. Add egg whites slowly. While beating, constantly add 1/4 tsp. anise oil. Spread on cooled cookies. Decorate with colored sugars, silver dragees, and cinnamon drops.

From Adrienne Svozil of Ramsey, New Jersey:

I was an immigrant who came to America with my mother on June 21, 1922. I was two years old; she was thirty-five.

This recipe for "Kaymak" was my mother's and not known by most Middle-Easterners. My mother and I are of Armenian background.

"Kaymak," by the way, is a non-sweet cream placed on top of the kadayiff, or paklova (layers of filo dough, honey, walnuts, etc.), the recipe for which is found in many cookbooks. But the topping or, "Kaymak," is not found easily in recipe books.

KAYMAK

1 quart or 1 pint heavy cream (1 quart serves 18-20, 1 pint serves 8-10).

Boil cream on <u>very slow</u> fire for 2 hours, after which place pan in warm place (oven - don't have oven on) for 2 hours. Use 8" x 8" cake pan or 2 of them or 1 large pan. Then set in refrigerator for 8 hours or overnight. After this, with a sharp knife, delicately cut loose bubbles which may have risen and set. Cut 1" wide strips; roll up and remove from liquid and onto a plate. Serve on top of paklava or kadayiff.

From Sandra Dorian Pizzano of West Des Moines, Iowa:

I received this recipe from my great-aunt Eugenie. She arrived in the U.S. by way of Ellis Island. She was a widow with a young son coming to America with hopes of making a new life. Our family has enjoyed this recipe for many years.

SEMETE (ARMENIAN COFFEE CAKE)

Combine in bowl:

4 cups or more all-purpose flour
1 tsp. baking powder
1/2 tsp. salt

Blend together:

1 egg
1/2 cup milk
1/2 lb. melted butter

Combine liquids with flour mixture while liquids are still warm. Mix and knead thoroughly, then shape a fistful of dough into cigar-like form. Bring ends together forming a circle about 3" - 4" in diameter. Set aside about 30 minutes. Then dip each "ring" in egg and coat with sesame seeds. Bake on cookie sheet 25-30 minutes.

From Connie Boger of Wichita, Kansas:

My father came to this country through Ellis Island from Greece at the age of sixteen. Mother found this a great way to "stretch" one chicken for nine people!

GREEK CHICKEN POULOFF

1 stewing hen
1 large onion, diced
1 #2 can tomatoes
1 8 oz. can tomato puree

salt & pepper, to taste
1 tsp. basil
1 tbsp. parsley
garlic, as desired

Add enough water to above to cook chicken until well done. Remove chicken. To liquid add 2/3 cup rice and enough liquid to cook rice. Remove chicken from bone and add to cooked rice mixture.

From Florence Collatos of Andover, Massachusetts:

Harry J. Kaniares came to the United States from a small village in the mountains of Greece in 1906. There was no school in the village and the children traveled all day to get to a school where they stayed for a week. They lived on the bread and cheese that they brought with them.

Seeing no future there, he left the village at age fourteen and came to the United States. He went to St. Louis where he had an uncle who had become successful in the candy business, but his uncle paid him so poorly he was walking around in the snow with holes in the soles of his shoes.

He left St. Louis and came to the Boston area where he shined shoes on the corner and saved enough money to open a shoeshine parlor and a cobbler shop. During this period he lived in a room with three other young men so he could save on expenses. Next, he opened an ice cream parlor and candy store, where he worked seven days a week and sent money home for dowries so that his sisters would be able to get good husbands. He brought his brother to the United States and gave him the shoeshine parlor. He then opened a high-class restaurant with gourmet food.

In the store next to the restaurant there was a pretty, young lady working as a clerk. He courted her for six years by buying two tickets a week for her and her sister to go to the movies so she would not be tempted to go out with another man while he was working. They were married when he had saved enough money to pay cash for a house.

He continued to open restaurants and used the profits to build commercial buildings while living well and being generous to his family, the community, and the folks back home in the village.

At age fifty-two, his wife suffered a paralyzing stroke, and he retired to take care of her, leaving his two sons in charge of the business. With his care and devotion, she recovered almost fully, and they were able to have twenty years of retirement and travel while living on his investments.

This following recipe is one of the favorite ones he made for his family, which he learned from his mother back in the village in Greece.

It is served in Greek restaurants here, but it's not quite as good as Dad's soup.

GREEK EGG LEMON SOUP

1 chicken for broth (3 quarts)
1 cup rice
4 eggs
juice of 3 lemons

Boil a chicken for broth. Cook 1 cup of rice. Add rice to 3 quarts of chicken broth.

Separate 4 eggs. Beat egg whites until foamy.
Beat egg yolks and add juice of 3 lemons. Beat again.

Mix yolk-lemon mixture to egg whites by beating. Slowly add broth into egg mixture, 1 ladle at a time while beating. When half of broth has been beaten in, add all the rest of the broth and rice and stir.

From Teena Grosinski of Mineola, New York:

My mother's name is Reveka Lakis. She came to America from the island of Cyprus in July 1930.

CHICK PEAS AND SPINACH

1 small onion
1 can chick peas (19 oz.)
2 tbsp. oil
2 tbsp. tomato paste
1 can spinach (15 oz.), drained
juice of 1/2 lemon or 2 tbsp.
salt & pepper, to taste

Saute diced onion in oil in saucepan. Add undrained chick peas. Bring to boil and add rest of ingredients. Reduce to low. Simmer for 15-20 minutes. It is simple and nutritious.

From Jacqueline A. Frost Deasy of Port Jefferson, New York:

My grandfather's name was Nicholas Melissinos. My grandmother was Daisy Welsh Melissinos, and my mother was Chrisula Melissinos Frost.

My Greek grandfather and English grandmother arrived at Ellis Island in 1904. They had met and married in London, England, and came over with their first child, a two-year old daughter, Chrisula. When the immigration procedures were over they found themselves finally on the New York City dock and hadn't the vaguest notion of how to get in touch with Greek friends in the city or where they were located. My grandfather decided to leave my grandmother and the baby on the dock by the luggage and go find his friends' neighborhood so they could temporarily settle in.

Because he had trouble finding the area he was looking for, my grandfather took several hours to locate the address he had carried with him from London. When he finally arrived back on the dock, there was my grandmother and their daughter sound asleep on top of the pile of luggage on the, by now, empty dock and totally unaware of their surroundings. My grandfather repeated the story many times -- the picture of them huddled together asleep on the luggage amused and impressed him so strongly.

This is a Greek recipe from my grandfather.

LAMB AND MACARONI

leg of lamb - any size
large can of whole tomatoes
1 pound Dtalini macaroni, #39 or #40
salt
pepper
smidgen of oregano
small cuts of garlic

Salt and pepper top of lamb, cut and insert small garlic pieces in top fatty skin. Roast lamb in a 350° oven for 1 1/2 hours (to your taste). When cooked, take lamb out of roasting pan and put aside covering with foil to keep warm. Keep the oven on at 400°. Put roasting pan with meat juices on burner on top of stove; add can of tomatoes (breaking tomatoes down with a fork); add approximately 1/2 can of water, seasonings, and heat till simmering point (on medium heat). When simmering, add macaroni, stir and immediately take off the stove and put into oven for a total of 20 minutes -- stirring once after 10 minutes in the oven. Meanwhile, carve lamb so that all is ready at once and serve immediately.

From Irene Knowles of Palm Beach Gardens, Florida:

My mother, Maria Tsardoulias, came through Ellis Island in 1916 from Samos, Greece.

I have a favorite recipe of my mother called Diples. The unusual thing about her recipe is how this pastry looks when it is finished. It looks like large roses.

In Greece they use ashes from wood to put in the dough to make it light and fluffy!

Samos is one of the larger islands near Asia Minor and Turkey. Pythagoras, the mathematician, lived on Samos. They make good wine on this island, but you have to go there to get it.

GREEK DIPLES (ROSES)

6 eggs
1/4 cup butter, melted & cooled
1 tsp. finely shredded orange peel
1/4 cup orange juice
2 tbsp. brandy
2 1/2 - 3 cups all-purpose flour
1 tsp. baking powder
cooking oil for deep frying
1 cup honey
2 tbsp. water
ground cinnamon
3/4 cup ground walnuts

In small mixer bowl beat eggs at high speed on electric mixer about 4 minutes or till thick and lemon colored. Stir in butter, orange peel, orange juice & brandy. Stir together 2 cups of the flour and the baking powder. Stir into egg mixture.

Stir in as much of the remaining flour as you can mix in using a spoon. On a lightly floured surface, knead in remaining flour to make a moderately stiff dough. Continue kneading till dough is smooth and elastic (about 5-8 minutes).

Roll out dough very thin. Cut entire length long strips. Drop 1 strip into hot oil (360°). Use long-handled fork. Slip dough between tines of a long-tined fork and twist dough quickly into a rose shape using a second fork to guide the dough. Continue cooking till rose is lightly browned. Transfer to paper towels. Repeat with remaining dough.

Just before serving, combine water and honey in a saucepan. Heat till warm. Pour over the roses in the platter. Sprinkle with cinnamon and walnuts.

To keep rose from coming apart (while cooking), the tail end of the dough is tucked into the center of the rose.

From Jeanette Farha Bayouth of Wichita, Kansas:

My father, Henry Saed Farha, arrived on August 16, 1920, to Ellis Island on the U.S. Philadelphia from Jdaidat Marj'ayoun, Lebanon. His eight-year old sister, Raifa, was detained on Ellis Island for nine months until her eyes cleared from trachoma.

CABBAGE ROLLS

<u>Stuffing for Cabbage or Grape Leaves</u>

2 cups ground beef, coarsely
 ground
1 cup rice
1 tbsp. salt

1 tsp. cinnamon
1/4 tsp. pepper
2 tbsp. butter

Wash rice, add meat, butter, and seasoning and mix well.

<u>Cabbage</u>

Choose a soft, loose head of cabbage. Boil enough water in a large pan with 2 tbsp. salt to cover cabbage. Remove core from bottom center of cabbage with a knife. Separate cabbage leaves and drop into boiling water for 3-5 minutes. Remove leaves from water when wilted and place in a pan until cool enough to handle. Slice off heavy rib on leaves. If leaves are large, cut in half. Lay small pieces of cabbage in bottom of 2 or 3-quart pan to cover bottom. Place a heaping tbsp. of rice and meat filling on each cut leaf and roll firmly. Lay cabbage rolls neatly in rows, making several layers. Place 3 garlic cloves among these layers. Put some leftover cabbage leaves over the top layer of cabbage rolls. Place a saucer, for weight on top. Put 1 1/2 cups water with 1 tsp. salt and juice from 2 lemons over cabbage rolls or enough to barely cover. Bring to a boil. Reduce heat, cook on low for 1 hour.

GRAPELEAVES

Pick fresh grape leaves (wild ones do not bear grapes but have tender leaves) or buy a jar commercially.

Wash leaves, separate, place leaf vein side up; stuff by placing meat mixture in the leaf, folding sides over and rolling up. It's good to put lamb bones, chicken thighs, on bottom of pan. Then cover with several rolls of rolled grape leaves. Place a heavy saucer dish on top, cover with water, add 1/2 cup lemon juice. Bring to a boil, reduce heat, cook on slow fire for 1 hour. Serve by draining and saving the juice, then invert pan on a large round platter. Garnish with lemon wedges.

From Willie Mike of Marshall, Texas:

TABOOLY SALAD

1 cup mint, chopped	6 large tomatoes
1 cup cracked wheat, fine	1/2 cup lemon juice
1 bunch green onions	1/2 cup salad oil
1 bunch parsley	salt & pepper, to taste

Soak cracked wheat in water for 15 minutes. Drain dry. Dice all ingredients and cut parsley in small pieces with kitchen shears. Mix all well. Serve on lettuce leaves. Fill cup with salad and turn over on lettuce leaves. Garnish with fresh mint and black olives. Serves 4.

S.S. PHILADELPHIA

From Georgianna Nicola Rishwain of Stockton, California:

My grandmother, Nazera Maloof Nicola, was one of those early immigrants in the early 1900's. She loved America with all her heart. She proudly flew the American flag and stood up and saluted every time she heard the Star Spangled Banner played on TV or the radio. This was made for festive occasions, especially Easter.

ROOZ IB HALEEB (RICE PUDDING)

2 quarts milk
3/4 cup raw rice
1/2 cup sugar
2 tbsp. cornstarch

Bring milk to boil. Wash and drain rice, add to milk, stirring occasionally for approximately 15 minutes. Add sugar and cornstarch (dissolve in small amount of cold water). Stir and cook for about 15 more minutes, or until rice is well done. Pour into dessert dishes and cool to room temperature. Can sprinkle with cinnamon if desired. Serves 8.

From Deana Solomon of Flushing, Michigan:

My mother's name was (Assyrian origin) Salby (Benjamin) Koshaba. She and my brother Carl came to this country by way of Ellis Island in December 1916 from Turkey.

My father came to this country also by way of Ellis Island from Turkey in 1912. His name was John Koshaba.

MEATBALL SOUP

1 lb. ground beef
1 cup green onions, finely chopped
1 cup (fine) cracked wheat
1/2 tsp. salt
1/2 tsp. black pepper
2 tbsp. oil

In 3-quart pot, brown 1/2 cup green onions with 2 tbsp. oil. Then add 2 quarts water, salt & pepper and bring to boil. Then add 1/2 cup cracked wheat.

In large bowl mix together: 1 lb. ground beef, 1/2 cup green onions, 1/2 cup cracked wheat. Make into 2" meat balls. Drop into pot, bring to boil again, then lower heat to medium and cover and cook for about 45 minutes. Serves about 5.

From Mrs. Victoria Farishian of Leonia, New Jersey:

My parents were born in Turkey and entered America through Ellis Island. Soud Kebah is one of our family's favorite recipes.

SOUD KEBAH

2 lbs. chopped lamb
1 1/2 cups bulgour (cracked wheat #3)
4 cups lamb or beef broth
1/2 cup crushed, dried mint
1 tsp. paprika
salt & pepper, to taste

Mix all together -- make large balls (size of medium orange) with a little cold water. Cook in broth for 45 minutes on low flame. Serve with scallions if you prefer.

ENGLAND
IRELAND
SCOTLAND
WALES

From Mrs. Roma Hunt Hotaling of Cresskill, New Jersey:

The Hunt family arrived from England in 1921. My father, Albert, came six months ahead so he could find a job and a place to live. Effie, Donald, and I came after my father got settled.

My mother was known among her friends for her roast beef and Yorkshire Pudding and, most of all, her mince pies. She always made small ones in little tins. They can also be made in cupcake tins or as regular-size pies.

MINCE MEAT PIE

1/2 lb. brown sugar
1/2 lb. kidney beef suet, cut up
1 lb. apples, grated
1/2 lb. currants
1/2 lb. each of brown and white raisins
1/4 lb. shelled almonds (skinless), chopped
1/4 lb. lemon, orange and citron peel
1/2 tsp. nutmeg
1/2 tsp. allspice
1 lemon, juice and rind
2 tbsp. brandy (more if desired)

Mix all together and put in jars and keep in refrigerator and use as desired. This will make 3 1/2 lbs. of mincemeat for many 9" pies. Cup cake tins can be used to make dozens of small ones and pastry can be used on the top and bottom. A crumb topping might be preferred.

YORKSHIRE PUDDING

1 cup milk
1 cup sifted all-purpose flour
1 tsp. salt

2 eggs, well-beaten
1/4 cup drippings from meat

After taking the roast beef from the oven (450°) pour some of the drippings in each cup cake pan. Mix 2 well-beaten eggs with 1 cup of milk and add to dry ingredients. Beat until smooth. Pour batter into 12 cup cake pans. Bake at 450° for 20 minutes. No longer. Serve with gravy. Makes 1 dozen.

From Margaret Ellen Sims Miller of Vernal, Utah:

I am submitting two recipes from my English grandmother, Elizabeth Makinson Sims, who came through Ellis Island in 1926 from Wigan, Lancashire, England. My dad and grandfather also passed through this place-of-sorting-out before entrance into this land of freedom and opportunity. They immigrated due to the 1926 mine strike and came here for work at Rock Springs, Wyoming, in the coal mines there. However, upon reaching their destination they found a better and safer opportunity, working for the Union Pacific Railroad in Green River, Wyoming, where they lived for most of their lives. I still have in my possession the tag worn by my father, Edmund Sims, Jr., placed on his person when being processed and examined for entry into the U.S.

These recipes were written in my grandmother's own handwriting. I cherish these greatly.

LEMON PUDDING

1 1/2 lemons, juice and grated
 rind
1 cup sugar
1/3 cup all-purpose flour
1/4 tsp. salt

2 egg yolks
1 cup milk
1 tbsp. melted butter
2 stiffly beaten egg whites

Beat egg yolks, lemon and milk. Mix flour, sugar, salt, and add to the first mixture. Add melted butter and fold in stiffly beaten egg whites. Bake for 65 minutes in a slow oven in a baking dish set in pan of water. Makes pudding and sauce.

GINGER SNAPS OR "LONDON CURLS"

4 oz. self-rising flour
4 oz. golden syrup (I believe this must be brown karo syrup)
4 oz. butter
1/4 oz. ginger
juice of half of lemon

Melt butter, sugar, lemon juice slowly in a sauce pan until all melted. Add flour and ginger sifted together and warm gently, but do not cook! Remove from heat and place tsp. of mixture 3 " apart on a <u>well-greased</u> baking sheet. Bake in a moderate oven (370°) until done. Curl over end of spoon when taking them off the pan (leave for a few seconds after removing pan from oven before curling).

From Carol M. Rapson of East Lansing, Michigan:

This is an English recipe, and the loaves are a beautiful golden brown.

SAFFRON BREAD

1/16 oz. saffron
1 envelope active, dry yeast (1/4 oz.)
1/2 tsp. sugar
2 cups sugar
7 1/2 cups all-purpose flour
1 tsp. salt
a little nutmeg
3/4 lb. shortening (can be lard, crisco,
 margarine, or any combination of your choice)
2 cups raisins, washed
1 tsp. lemon extract (not imitation)
1 egg, slightly beaten

Crumble saffron fine and pour 1/2 cup boiling water over it. Steep at least 2 hours. Make a sponge mixture of yeast in 1/2 cup warm water with the 1/2 tsp. sugar. Add this yeast mixture to 2 1/2 cups flour and add more warm water -- just enough to be able to beat it a little with a tablespoon. Cover and place in a warm place for about an hour. In a large bowl, put about 5 cups flour, salt and nutmeg. Work in shortening. Add 2 cups sugar, mixing in well, then raisins. Add to sponge mixture, lemon extract and egg and the saffron mixture. Mix and add a little more warm water, if necessary, until right consistency. Place in warm place until double in size. Shape into buns or bread loaves and put into greased pans. Let rise until doubled; bake at 375° for 15-20 minutes or until golden brown.

From Judy O'Leary Anderson of Syracuse, New York:

Here is a treasured recipe for Irish Sodabread made by my mother, Nellie T. O'Donoghue O'Leary, who came through Ellis Island in 1920 from the village of Rathmore, County Kerry, Ireland.

My mother was a remarkable woman who was loved and admired by everyone who knew her. Hers was the typical Irish story: a marriage arranged for the only son in the family necessitating in the three daughters leaving the farm to find positions elsewhere. She was sponsored by an uncle and immigrated to the U.S.A. She was hired to work in the home of a prominent Buffalonian.

From an early age on, we knew that our mother was someone special. In the early 1930's, it wasn't unusual to walk into our back hall and see a homeless victim of the Depression eating on the steps.

Every holiday we would have one or two children from a local orphanage joining in our celebration (we could never understand why they always wanted to stay inside the house instead of going out to play). More often than not we'd have an elderly neighbor too, and many's the time we'd have to deliver a basket with a hot turkey dinner in it to an ill or confined neighbor before we sat down to our own. We'd take turns doing it. There were six children in our family, but there was always enough food to share.

Mom was always there when there was a need. During the war she rolled bandages and worked for the Ladies of Charity, sewing and making clothes for poor children. She was the one who walked door-to-door, collecting money for the March of Dimes and signing up neighbors to give blood and/or donations for other worthwhile organizations. If there was a fund-raiser for the church or school she was either in the kitchen cooking the dinner or working at the bake sale or card party.

She was an excellent cook, and whenever Confirmation was held in her parish, the pastor would call her to come and cook the dinner for the Bishop.

Every St. Patrick's Day, after the parade, we would have about thirty people squeezed into our little flat for a ham and corned beef and cabbage dinner with Irish Sodabread and tea. She was the spearhead in welcoming new "greenhorns" and getting together the members and friends of her Irish family. She would organize picnics and parties so that they would have a sense of belonging in their new country.

Although she had little education herself, she saw to it that her six children had an excellent education.

My mother was a woman of deep faith, a devoted wife and mother, and a loving, caring person. Anyone who ever knew her would attest to the fact that she touched their lives in a way they would never forget!

NELLIE O'LEARY'S IRISH SODABREAD

4 cups all-purpose flour
1 cup sugar
4 tsp. baking powder
1/2 tsp. salt
1 stick melted butter

1 1/2 cups raisins
2 tbsp. caraway seeds
1 1/2 cups buttermilk
1 egg, slightly beaten
1/3 tsp. baking soda

Sift flour, salt, baking powder, and sugar; add melted butter and mix. Stir in raisins and caraway seeds. Combine buttermilk, egg, and baking soda. Make a well in the center of the batter. Pour liquid ingredients and stir into flour mixture. Place in large iron frying pan, well-buttered. Use a knife to make a cross on the top. Moisten with melted butter. Bake in a 375° oven for an hour, or until golden brown and shrinks from the side of the pan.

From Ruth Pecoy of Rockwell City, Iowa:

This recipe is from my great-grandmother who came over on "Coffin Ships" from Ireland, from the Harbor of Cobh.

COLCANNON

2 cups shredded cabbage
4 servings leftover mashed potatoes
6 green onions, chopped
2 tbsp. butter
1 tbsp. parsley flakes
pinch of white pepper

Cook cabbage in a little salted water in a covered saucepan 5 minutes - drain well. To the mashed potatoes, add drained cabbage, onions, butter, parsley flakes and pepper. Warm in a skillet, over very low heat, stirring frequently. Makes 4-5 servings.

This is a typical Irish dish, cherished by this lover of the "Auld Sod."

CARAMEL DUMPLINGS

Syrup

2 cups sugar
3 cups hot water
1 tbsp. butter
pinch of salt

Dumplings
scant 1/2 cup butter
1 tbsp. sugar
1 cup milk
2 tsp. baking powder
2 cups flour
1 egg

Syrup: Melt 1/2 cup sugar in 8" x 11" cake pan. Add 3 cups hot water, butter, rest of sugar and salt.

Dumplings: Mix ingredients well and drop by tbsp. in hot syrup. Bake 20 minutes in 350° oven.

This is truly an old recipe, designed to satisfy the sweet tooth of the children of pioneer days.

From Mrs. William Moran, Sr. of Merrillville, Indiana:

My mother, Winifred Greene from Galway, came to this country in 1909. My father, Steven Nolan, arrived in America about the same time. They married years later. As time passed, we eight enjoyed "A Boiled Dinner."

A BOILED DINNER

1 lb. of plate beef
1 medium turnip, cubed
1 bunch of carrots, sliced
6 to 8 peeled potatoes
1 medium yellow onion
salt & pepper, to taste
2 quarts water

Place the plate beef in a heavy aluminum pan or a dutch oven. Have about 1" of fat on the meat. Brown it slowly for 20 minutes, turning often. The onions should be added also. Add 2 quarts of water and let it simmer for 2 1/2 hours. Season with salt and pepper, to taste. Now, add all of the vegetables and cook another 30 minutes. Serve on a large platter, surrounded by vegetables; some might like to use a little mustard. A luncheon of beef soup might be served the next day; after refrigeration, any fat could be skimmed off.

From Mary V. Lee of Deer Park, New York:

This recipe was handed down by my Irish great-grandmother to my grandmother to my mother. We had red cabbage every blessed Sunday to the delight of my immigrant father from Italy, who could not get enough of it. My mother introduced him to other dishes, but red cabbage was his favorite.

RED CABBAGE

1 whole cabbage, cored and shredded
1 tsp. salt
1 medium apple, peeled, cored and sliced
1 sprinkle sugar
1 small onion, sliced
2 strips of bacon
1 tsp. vinegar
1 cup water
5 ginger snaps, crumbled

In large pot, put in bacon and cook until crispy. Add onion and saute until soft. Remove bacon and drain, put aside. Put cabbage in pot and the rest of ingredients except ginger snaps. Bring to a boil and let simmer until cabbage is just about done. Add ginger snaps and cook until done. Sprinkle bacon on just before serving.

* Household Hint: Put one tbsp. cream of tartar in with cabbage. It will release the acid in cabbage. For people who have trouble eating cabbage, it will help.

Hope you enjoy !

From Ruth Stallbaum Coleman of Moyock, North Carolina:

With soft drinks a billion dollar industry today, we wonder how the immigrant kids kept bubbly and cool. They made oceans of lemonade--just one lemon rolled and softened went a long way. But my mother, Ethelinda, poured water again and again over oatmeal (dry) until the result was "Oat Milk." This was flavored to taste with vanilla and sugar and served cold. What a nourishing treat ! Arriving at Ellis Island on the Vessel Astoria in 1901 was a family of twelve.

All that were eligible filed on homesteads in western South Dakota where my mother met my father, August Heinrich Frederich Stallbaum, born June 10, 1879, in Heiligenhafen, Germany. He was fourteen years old when his schoolmaster arranged for an Iowa farmer to pay his passage (indentured servitude). Daddy first filed on a homestead in Kansas, but because there was a drought there that year, he pulled up stakes and filed on a homestead in western South Dakota, where there was a natural spring.

From Patricia Devlin Regan of Rockville Centre, New York:

Here is my grandmother's recipe for what she called "Poverty Cake"...no doubt because it required no eggs, butter or milk.

My grandparents came to New York in 1892 on a sailing vessel called the "Servia" from Liverpool, England. My grandmother told me that the crossing took <u>five</u> weeks and that she was so terribly sea sick she prayed for "the ship to go down." I'm sure they traveled in steerage class. I was told that when they neared New York, a doctor (either on board or on Ellis Island) wanted to vaccinate all the children. Not knowing what the word "vaccination" meant, my grandmother hid her two children!

POVERTY CAKE

2 cups water
2 cups raisins
1 cup sugar
1 tsp. cinnamon
1 full tsp. "plus a little bit" of cloves
2 tbsp. lard

Boil the above ingredients for 3 minutes and then cool. When cool, add:

2 cups all-purpose flour
1 tsp. baking soda

Beat about 200 strokes, until mixture is bubbly. Bake in tin loaf pan which has been greased and floured. Bake for 1 hour in hot oven, then reduce heat until cake is done (about 15 more minutes).

From Robert McCorristin of Millville, New Jersey:

This is a favorite family recipe that was brought from Ireland and has been enjoyed by our family for many years.

JERSEY CLAM PIE

pastry for two-crust pie
1/2 cup chopped onion
6 tbsp. butter
1/2 cup all-purpose flour
3 cups clam juice (save juice from clams)
4 cups chopped clams (chowder size)
5 oz. frozen peas
chopped canned pimento
2 cups chopped potatoes

Prepare pastry.

Cook onion in butter till tender. Blend flour, 1 tsp. salt, add all other ingredients. Cook until potatoes are tender then add pepper to taste. Pour into prepared pastry and bake at 450° for 20 to 25 minutes.

From Edith Gassman of Attica, New York:

We ate these oatcakes at any time of day. They weren't reserved for special meals -- just part of our daily food. Scotch oatmeal must be used. This is a coarse, gritty meal -- very small grains that don't soften when cooked. There's no food more delicious and satisfying.

The receipt for my grandmother's passage shows it was prepaid by her husband, Robert B. Meek, who was already in America. It is dated August 18, 1887, and is for "Mary Meek and others" -- their five children -- from Glasgow to Buffalo. It was #R1251, issued by J.W. Klauck, agent for the State Steamship Co, (Lim) -- Ocean Class Steerage -- at a cost of $108.00 !!

A blessing on what we were about to receive and a thank you for the bounty already received was given to God every time we ate -- whether it be an oatcake or scone and a cup of tea or a full meal of leg of lamb or mutton stew. God was always present.

SCOTCH OATCAKE

1 cup scotch oatmeal
1 tbsp. butter
1/2 cup hot water
dash of salt

Put the butter into the water and salt -- then pour this mixture over the oatmeal. Works together. Flatten with hand as thinly as possible into a round. The thinner, the better. Cut into wedges. Cook quickly for a few seconds in a hot griddle. Then place in a <u>very</u> <u>slow</u> oven until nicely browned and the edges curl up. Serve warm with butter, but delicious cold, buttered. Store in a tin box.

From Gladys E. Young of Lansing, Michigan:

I believe my father, James Harvey, and his brother Bill immigrated in 1919. He was seventeen and his brother was fourteen. They came to an uncle's farm in Bangar, Michigan, and were supposed to help on the farm.

As a young child, I remember him always going to night school to better himself and make a better life for his family.

He was a remarkable man and a real inspiration not only to his family but to a great many other people.

SPICE

1 cup brown sugar	1/2 tsp. cinnamon
1/2 cup crisco	1/2 tsp. nutmeg
2 eggs	1/4 tsp. ginger
1 cup sour milk	1/4 tsp. allspice
1 tsp. soda	raisins
2 cups all-purpose flour	
1 tsp. baking powder	
1 tsp. salt	

Mix ingredients together, then add spices. Bake at 350° for 45 minutes.

From Mrs. Patricia Scott Garmon of Escondido, California:

This is a recipe of my grandmother, Mary Agnes Teeley Fallon Scott.

Mary Agnes Teeley, born 1869, County Wicklow, Ireland, passed through Ellis Island in the year 1887 as the wife of Patrick Fallon (Falloon). Patrick died and she married Walter Scott. Thus, she was an expert in both Irish and Scottish cooking. Biscuits were her specialty, but the recipe is buried with her.

SCOTTISH SHORTBREAD

Cream together 3\4 cup butter (do not substitute for butter)
1\2 cup sugar
2 cups all-purpose flour

Put in 2 cake pans and press down with your hand. Mark in 8 wedges. Bake 35 to 40 minutes at 350° until lightly browned.

From Mrs. Philip Reefer of Humboldt, Iowa:

On August 28, 1920, my mother, along with my grandparents and her brother, left from Cardiff, South Wales, for a new land. They sailed on the S.S. Imperator, a prize of WW1 captured by the English from Germany. It was a favorite of the Kaiser and the largest vessel afloat at that time. They arrived five days later in New York Harbor.

Immigrants were held on board because it was Saturday. The dock hands did not work till Monday. That day being Labor Day, they were kept until Tuesday.

In Frances Mary Needs Eubank's autobiography she wrote:

> *"We were taken by ferry boat to Ellis Island and got a perfect view of the Statue of Liberty. What a memorable sight she was with her torch held high. We had heard so much about her. What a thrill it was!"*

> *"We were examined and when given a clean bill of health were given colored tickets on our lapels. On them was the name of our destination and the train we were to board. Many were not as fortunate as we and could not read, write, or understand English. They were shrewd and soon learned to follow those with the same color tickets, thus getting on the right train."*

My mother, Frances Mary Needs was one proud lady of her new home, America. She never had a desire to ever return to the land where she was born. This has been handed down and is now being made by the fourth generation of our family. They are a Good Friday tradition and I can't remember a Good Friday without them. Grandpa Needs was a miner in Wales and carried the warm buns to the mines inside his jacket for lunch.

HOT CROSS BUNS

Mix:

1/2 cup sugar
3 tbsp. butter
1/2 tsp. salt
1 pkg. active dry yeast (1/4 oz.)
1 cup milk & 1/4 cup water,
  heated to luke warm

Add:

1 egg, beaten
3 cups all-purpose flour
1/2 tsp. cinnamon
1/2 cup currants (or raisins)

Mix well. Cover, let rise until double in bulk. Shape into 2 dozen buns. Place in two 9" x 13" greased pans. Let rise about 1 hour. Brush with another slightly beaten egg. Cut a cross (+) in top of each bun with sharp knife or scissor. Bake in 400° oven for 20 minutes. Cool. When cool, fill crosses with powdered sugar frosting.

S.S. IMPERATOR

From Nancy Nyholm of Chicago, Illinois:

My mother, Frida Nielsen, was born in Bronderslev, Denmark, on March 10, 1898. She came to America in the early 1900's and went through Ellis Island. From there, she went directly to Miami, Florida, to work as a housekeeper for her sponsor who was a family member on her father's side. She was well known as a good cook.

KLEJNER (COOKIE)

4 egg yolks
2 egg whites
2 tbsp. butter
1/2 pint whipped cream

1 cup sugar
1 1/2 jiggers brandy
a little cardamon flavoring
flour, enough to roll out

Mix ingredients in order given to make workable dough. Roll out thin. Cut with pastry cutter into 1" x 4" strips, make 1" slit in center and pull one end through slit. Fry in deep fat, very hot, and turn until browned evenly. Drain on unwaxed paper.

DANISH LIVERPASTE

2 lbs. liver
1/2 lb. fresh pork fat
1 lb. bacon, sliced
1 large or 2 small onions
1/4 lb. butter
1 cup all-purpose flour

3 eggs
salt & pepper, to taste
allspice, about 1/2 tsp.
cloves, about 1/2 tsp.
touch of Worcestershire sauce

Grind fresh pork fat twice. Melt butter, gradually adding flour and milk (milk enough to form a paste). Add ground fat and let simmer until melted. Grind liver and onions twice. Mix fat and liver, eggs and spices. Line pan with bacon slices (both bottom and sides). Put in mixture and cover with sliced bacon. Bake 1 hour at 350°. Cool overnight. Slice and serve.

From Annette Andersen of Omaha, Nebraska:

This recipe is my mother's, Nadjeschda Overgaard, of Kimballton, Iowa. She is eighty-six years old, born in Siberia in 1905, of Danish parents.

Her father, Carl Lynge, was sent to Russia in the early 1900's to establish creameries by the Danish government. He returned to Denmark in 1904 to bring his new bride to live in Russia. The family came back to Denmark in 1910 just ahead of the Revolution.

Again, the father set off, this time to America to seek his fortune. In 1916, his wife, Anna, my mother, and two other children made the long journey to America, thus going through Ellis Island. The memory my mother has of Ellis Island as a child is "People, people everywhere, long lines, hysterical children, and much confusion and anxiety as everyone was checked for disease - they pushed us around like cattle."

ÆBLEKAGE (DANISH APPLE CAKE)

3 cups bread crumbs
1/4 cup butter
1/2 cup sugar
3 cups applesauce
1 cup whipping cream
2 tbsp. sugar
red jelly for decoration

Brown crumbs in skillet with butter and sugar. Arrange crumb mixture and applesauce in alternate layers on a serving dish. Chill. Whip cream with 2 tbsp. sugar and put on top of cooled mixture. Decorate with dabs of red jelly.

From Stella Svane of Rutherford, New Jersey:

My parents were both immigrants. My mother came from Germany, my father from Denmark. We lived in New York City on West 30th Street. My father worked for forty-five years for Consolidated Edison Co. In the 1920's, New York City was a wonderful place to raise a family. Our favorite spot was Central Park! For five cents we could take the subway to Coney Island .... and as children we did just that. We had no car, but our family was the first family on 30th Street to get a bathtub. In the summertime, we saw "Park Movies" given by the Hudson Guild Settlement House and held in Chelsea Park. You sat on newspaper, placed on the ground. The movies could not start until it got dark. As soon as that happened, the children would cheer, and the free movie would begin. It was a wonderful time to grow up in the city. My parents worked hard. The house on 30th Street was a rooming house. My mother rented out rooms to single people in need of a place to live. It was a simpler life, but as I look back, it was a good one.

BRUNE KAGER (LITTLE BROWN CAKES)

1/2 cup dark corn syrup
5 tbsp. dark brown sugar
4 tbsp. unsalted butter
1/2 tsp. baking soda
1 1/2 cups all-purpose flour
1 tsp. powdered cloves
1 1/4 tsp. ground cardamon
1 1/4 tsp. grated lemon peel
3 ounces almonds, blanched and peeled

Heat the corn syrup, brown sugar and butter in heavy saucepan until the sugar is thoroughly dissolved. Do not let it boil. Remove from heat and let it cool. Meanwhile, sift the baking soda, flour, powdered cloves together in large bowl. Add the cardamon, grated lemon peel, and the lukewarm syrup and knead dough well by pressing it down with the heel of your hand, turning it, folding it over and pressing again. Continue kneading for 5 to 10 minutes until the dough is smooth and shiny. Wrap in wax paper and set aside in a cool place for at least 2 hours. Preheat oven to 400°. On a lightly floured surface, roll dough into a sheet 1/8" thick, then, with a cookie cutter or a small wine glass, cut into 2" rounds. Grease a cookie sheet and lay cookies on it about 1" apart. Lightly press 1 almond into the center of each and bake about 5 or 6 minutes or until they are a light gold. Cool the Brune Kager on the cookie sheet. The cookies can be stored for several weeks in a tightly sealed tin. Makes 6 dozen cookies.

From Gus Kaikkonen of New York, New York:

These are my Aunt Ida Kaikkonen Dewey's reminiscences of her mother, Wilhemina Untinen Kaikkonen, who arrived at Ellis Island just after the turn of the century:

>"Mother didn't use recipes but she was a wonderful cook. Did you know she was the head cook for Czar Nicholas when Pa was in the Russian army? I don't know what they called her. I made some fruit soup yesterday. Put about a cup of prunes, a little less of dried apricots and raisins to soak a few hours, in enough water (and a rounded tablespoon of sugar) so they're well covered. I cooked them twenty minutes to a half hour and thickened it with two heaping teaspoons of potato starch, dissolved in water (as for gravy thickening). I cook by taste as Mother did.

>Pa came here in the late 1890's. Probably because of his artistic ability, he got work decorating homes for the rich on Long Island. He mixed his own paints and made his own stencils for the fancy work. He did so well that within a year he had bought and furnished a lovely home in Newark, New Jersey (furnished largely with stuff from these Long Island homes), and sent Mother money for her passage.

>She, with Arthur and baby David, were living in an apartment in Helsinki. When the letter came, the "Campania" was leaving for America via Britain in half a day, so she sublet the apartment, packed, and got herself and the children on it.

>It was a three-week voyage. She made the acquaintance of another woman with children and worked very hard learning her language so she could talk some "American" when she arrived. When they got to Ellis Island, the other woman couldn't talk "American" either. Mother had learned Italian."

My Aunt Anne told me that due to work, my grandfather was unable to meet my grandmother when she arrived--apparently being met made it easier to leave Ellis Island. Instead, he sent a friend with her picture. Grandma saw this man nodding and waving at her and ignored him because she suspected the worst, but finally, unable to find her husband and afraid she'd be detained, she waved back and made the officials understand that this stranger was her husband. She was released to him, and it was a great relief when he introduced himself as her husband's friend.

PULLA (A FINNISH BREAD)

1 package active, dry yeast (1/4 oz.)
1/4 cup warm water
3/4 cup warm milk
1/2 cup sugar
1/2 tsp. salt

2 eggs
1 tsp. ground cardamom
approx. 4 1/2 cups all-purpose flour
1/2 cup melted butter

Combine yeast with water. Set aside and after a few moments blend in milk, sugar, salt, eggs, cardamom and 2 cups of the flour. Beat until smooth. Add butter and blend well. Stir in 2 1/4 more cups of flour beating to make a dough.

Coat a board with the remaining flour, turn dough out on the board. Scoop up flour and pat it over the surface of the dough. Knead until smooth and satiny feeling (5-10 minutes).

Place the dough in a buttered bowl and turn it to grease the outside. Cover and let rise in a warm place until doubled in bulk (1 - 1 1/2 hours).

Knead again. Divide dough into 6 equal portions and fashion them into long strands. Using 3 strands per loaf shape dough into 2 braids. Place in lightly buttered loaf pans, and let rise again for 30 minutes, until dough is puffy looking. Brush with egg. Sprinkle generously with granulated sugar. Bake at 350° for approximately 25 minutes.

From Jim Fobel of New York, New York:

My grandfather, George Einar Wahlstrom, left Helsinki at age twenty-one and arrived at Ellis Island in 1904. He was a very talented musician and was fortunate to have a teaching position waiting for him at Suomi College in Hancock, Michigan. It was (and still is) a Finnish school in a Finnish settlement.

At the time, my grandmother, Hilma Alina Heikkinen, also a Finn, was a student at the school. They met and fell in love. After a three-year courtship, they married and raised five daughters. My grandmother, four aunts, and mother, Airi Elli Katri, were great cooks and bakers. I learned much from them as I grew up. Here are three favorite family recipes that represent my culinary heritage.

KROPSUA (FINNISH DESSERT PANCAKE)

This is a simple and delicious dessert that can be thrown together at a moment's notice from ingredients on hand. It's a big dessert pancake that is meant to collapse as it is taken from the oven. In Finland it is served with lingonberries, but any fresh fruit, sugared ahead of time to draw the juice, or preserves will be just as tasty.

3 large eggs
3 tbsp. granulated sugar
pinch of salt
2 cups milk

1 cup all-purpose flour
1 tbsp. confectioners' sugar
fresh berries, fruit, or preserves

Preheat the oven to 425°. When it is hot, place a 9" cast-iron skillet or a cake pan in the oven and heat for 10 minutes. In a large bowl, whisk the eggs with the granulated sugar and salt. Whisk in the milk and then the flour to make a smooth batter. Carefully remove the hot pan from the oven with a potholder and lightly coat with vegetable oil. Pour in the batter all at once and bake for about 30 minutes, until puffed and golden brown. When removed from the oven, the pancake will collapse (this helps to make it creamy). Sift the confectioners' sugar over the top and serve hot, with berries, fruit or preserves. Makes 6 servings.

CARDAMOM COOKIES

These are the fragrant, crisp little cookies that I loved with cold milk as a child. Finns are partial to cardamom. I still recall how my mother took the little seeds from their pods, wrapped them in a linen napkin and pounded them with a hammer.

1 cup all-purpose flour
1/4 tsp. baking soda
1 tsp. ground cinnamon
1 tsp. ground cardamom

1 large egg
3/4 cup granulated sugar
8 tbsp. (1 stick) butter, melted

Preheat the oven to 350°. Grease and flour one or two baking sheets, tapping off the excess flour. In a medium bowl stir together the flour, baking soda, cinnamon and cardamom. In a large bowl, whisk the egg until frothy. Whisk in the sugar and butter. With a spoon, stir in the dry ingredients to make a batter. Using 1 tsp. of the batter for each cookie, spoon it onto the prepared baking sheet, about 2" apart. Bake about 12 minutes, or until lightly browned. With a spatula, transfer to a rack to cool. Use cooled sheets, lightly greased and floured as before, to bake the rest. Makes 5 to 6 dozen.

PUNAJUURISALAATTI (BEET AND CARROT SALAD)

You can add pickled herring to this salad though we never did at home when I was growing up. It has a bright, sunny color and light, pickled flavor. We serve it at all family get-togethers. Be sure to start the recipe a day before you want to serve it.

1 1/2 lbs. fresh beets (8 medium)
1 lb. carrots (8 medium), peeled
4 hard-cooked eggs
1 medium onion, grated
6 to 7 tbsp. cider vinegar
1 1/2 tsp. sugar
1/2 tsp. salt
1/4 tsp. pepper

Place the unpeeled beets in a large heavy saucepan and cover with cold water. Bring to a boil over high heat. Partially cover the pot and boil until tender, about 25 minutes. Drain and cool to room temperature. Place the carrots in a large pot and cover with cold water. Bring to a boil over high heat. Partially cover and cook until tender, about 10 minutes. Drain and cool to room temperature.

Using a paring knife or your fingertips, slip the skins from the beets. Cut beets and carrots into 1/2" dice and put them in a large bowl. Finely chop 3 of the eggs and add them to the beets and carrots. Add the grated onion, 6 tbsp. of the vinegar, the sugar, and the salt and pepper. Toss gently but thoroughly.

Bury the remaining whole egg in the center of the salad. Cover and refrigerate for 24 hours, tossing several times but keeping the whole egg covered.

To serve the salad, remove the buried egg (it will be a beautiful magenta color). Taste the salad and add the remaining tbsp. of vinegar, if desired. Mound the salad onto a shallow serving dish. Thinly slice the egg and arrange in an overlapping row across the center. Serve chilled. Makes 8 servings.

From Thordis K. Danielson of New Rockford, North Dakota:

My father, Lars M. Lee, was born in Brottum, Norway, in 1881 and came through Ellis Island in the early 1900's to seek a new, challenging life in America. He was a skilled wood craftsman and also was skillful and ingenious in working with his hands. Throughout his adulthood, he was engaged in fine carpentry and diversified farming in North Dakota. Our family had access to a large variety of meats, poultry, and fish, and our mother's method of preparation of foods was interesting and appealing. Rullepolse (meat roll) is one of our favorites and still is being prepared several generations later.

RULLEPOLSE (BEEF ROLL)

10" x 14" beef flank rectangle
several strips of beef
1 strip of beef suet
1 tbsp. salt
1/2 tsp. pepper
1 tsp. nutmeg
2 tsp. ginger
1 tbsp. chopped onion

Fill rectangular flank with beef and suet strips. Distribute spices and onion throughout strips. Roll tightly and sew open side and both ends with needle and heavy thread. Bind roll with stout string and secure well (this prevents breaking apart during cooking). Simmer in water until tender; place on tray, and press overnight using a heavy weighted object over meat roll in refrigerator. When pressed and chilled, remove cord and threads. Slice for meat tray or use in sandwich preparation. Beef stock may be used for soup base.

From Julia Anderson of Sioux City, Iowa:

My mother came from Trondhjem, Norway, in 1892. Jonah Buaas Rostad Anderson and daughter Laura Antonia, age two years. The husband and father, Markus Rostad Anderson, had come in 1890. They came to Sioux City, Iowa, and lived here the rest of their lives.

LAPSKAUS

1 lb. beef rib, boiled
1/2 lb. pork shoulder

salt & pepper, to taste
4 cups raw potatoes, cubed

Cube meat in 1" pieces. Cover well with water and cook till tender. Add potatoes to meat and cook till mushy. Four sliced weiners may be added the last few minutes.

From Eldoris Hustad of Granite Falls, Minnesota:

My husband's grandmother, Karoline Aarseth Hustad, brought this recipe with her from Norway in 1886. She was married to Iver Hustad on Christmas Eve the same year. They had eleven children.

They planted, harvested, and ate huge quantities of potatoes. Potato dumplings were served at least once a week in their home because the potatoes were readily available and cheap, and it kept the children busy grinding the potatoes.

For the past thirty years, my own family has made these same potato dumplings every Christmas Eve. We always make a double batch, and with the leftover dumplings, we slice and fry them in butter for our Christmas morning breakfast.

POTATO DUMPLINGS (KLUB)

6 cups ground raw potatoes
4 cups all-purpose flour
2 cups oatmeal

2 tsp. salt
chunks of salt pork or ham

Mix all ingredients except meat and form into snowball-size balls. Then press a chunk of meat into the center of each ball. Drop them into boiling water or ham broth. Simmer for about 45 minutes. Serve with butter.

From Gladys Granlund Hendrickson of Lake Park, Minnesota:

In August 1921, our family left the community of Langvassgrenda in Nordland, Norway. We were a family of four: my father, Peder Bang Larsen-Granlund, my mother, Astrid Dortea, my sister, Enne Adrianna, and I, Gladys Astrid. Since my father's brother, Bjorn, had settled at Fort Ransom, North Dakota, that was our destination. Two brothers were born at Fort Ransom: Peter and William Curtis. My father worked for thirty years as a mail carrier. My parents dreams were fulfilled as all four of their children graduated from college and were professionally employed. We four siblings now live in Florida, Washington, Colorado and Minnesota.

Here is an old favorite Norwegian recipe that was made for special occasions, especially Christmas.

SOTT SUPPE (SWEET SOUP)

Many prefer to eat this hot as a soup, but we preferred it as it cooled and congealed into a pudding served with cream or ice cream.

2 cups cranberry juice
2 cups grape juice
juice of 1 lemon (or 2 tbsp.)
4 tbsp. tapioca soaked in 1 cup water at
 least 4 hours
1 cup prunes
1 cup apricots
1 cup raisins
1/4 cup sugar
1 stick cinnamon
1/4 tsp. salt

Simmer for 30 minutes. Stir!!! (scorches easily!)
This makes about 15 small servings.

Delicious!!

From Liz Lorch of Spirit Lake, Iowa:

The following recipe is from my grandmother, Magda (Undem) Herigstad. She came to the United States from Stavanger, Norway, in 1915. She came to join her future husband, Garman Herigstad, who was a blacksmith in Roland, Iowa.

Until she married, she worked as a cook and housekeeper for the local church minister of Litchfield, Minnesota.

The Scandinavians are known for their rich dark breads, and my grandmother, missing this bread so much, tried to duplicate it. It is an original recipe that she developed after coming to the United States. In those days, you couldn't find this type of bread in Iowa where she lived after her marriage.

SCANDINAVIAN PUMPERNICKEL

16 oz. all brand buds
5 1/2 cups warm water
1 1/2 - 2 tbsp. salt
1/2 cup sorgum (you can use brown sugar or honey)
1 pkg. active, dry yeast (1/4 oz.)
1 tbsp. sugar
10-11 cups all-purpose flour

Mix together the first four ingredients and let soak for 15 minutes. Dissolve 1 pkg. dry yeast and 1 tbsp. sugar in 1/2 cup warm water. When the yeast and sugar are dissolved, add it to the bran mixture. Slowly add 10-11 cups white flour and knead well. You can start mixing the dough with a good mixer until dough becomes to stiff for the mixer. Cover with a damp cloth and let raise 1 - 1 1/2 hours. Knead again for about 10 minutes and add flour if dough seems too sticky. Divide into 3 loaves. Use greased bread pans or arrange loaves on a greased cookie sheet. Let rise again for 1 - 1 1/2 hours. You do not cover the loaves this time. Bake at 400° for 20 minutes. Then lower the oven temperature to 325° and bake for 1 1/2 hours. The crust of the bread will be very hard. Remove bread from the bread pans and cool on racks for at least 1/2 hour before cutting.

This bread is used for the famous Scandinavian open-faced sandwiches. Thin slices of the bread can be served with butter and any of the following toppings: salami, cheese, cold meats, cucumber, cold cooked sliced potatoes with chives or liver pate.

From Barbara Midland McCool of Thousand Oaks, California:

My mother, Arna Valand Midland, came to America from Mandal, Norway, in about 1929. She met and married my father, Chris Midland, also from Norway, (Spangereid), in Brooklyn. They lived in Brooklyn and raised their family there. This Kringle is a wonderful recipe that I still make very often for my family and friends.

MAMMA'S NORWEGIAN KRINGLE

3/4 lb. butter
2 pkgs. active dry yeast (1/4 oz. each)
3 1/2 cups all-purpose flour
1/2 cup sugar
1 tsp. ground cardamom
1 1/2 cups warmed milk
cinnamon
sugar
ground nuts

Melt 1/4 lb. butter in warmed milk. Mix all dry ingredients together. Add warmed milk/butter mixture to dry ingredients and mix well. Cover and let stand 1 hour in warm place to rise. Place dough on floured board and with rolling pin, roll out dough to about 1/4" thickness. Use 5 tbsp. butter (soft) and butter dough. Roll up, cover and let stand 15 minutes. Repeat last step. Let stand to rise 15 minutes. Repeat again with 6 tbsp. butter. Before rolling, sprinkle cinnamon, sugar and ground nuts. Roll into long tube shape in figure 8 or pretzel. Place on cookie sheet and allow to rise for 1 hour. Bake at 350° for 30 minutes or until golden brown. After cool, ice with following.

Icing

2 tbsp. butter
1 tsp. black coffee
confectioners' sugar to make a spreadable paste

Ice and top with more ground almonds or walnuts. Slice on diagonal and serve with coffee or tea. Freezes well, also.

From Rolf Nelson of Staten Island, New York:

My mother, Gunvor Kohler Nelson, arrived from Trondheim, Norway, in 1929 and settled in Brooklyn. Our family name had been Nielsen. My paternal grandfather was a sea captain, making frequent trips to England. After many difficult times trying to spell his name to the British, who were no doubt thinking of Lord Nelson, he finally relented and gave his name as Nelson.

A few years ago I tried to duplicate my mother's wonderful recipe for Kjot Suppe. I never mastered her method until she served it to me on a visit. While eating it, I bit into the ginger. This was the missing ingredient that made it so special.

KJOT SUPPE (MEAT SOUP)

2 lbs. beef, cut into serving portions or
 1/2 beef and 1/2 lamb (better taste)
2 quarts water
2 tsp. salt
1 medium onion, chopped
2 carrots, cut for soup
2 stalks of celery, cut for soup
1 cup yellow turnip, peeled and cubed
1 parsnip, peeled and cut for soup
1/2 cup parsley, finely chopped
1 small piece ginger (size of teaspoon bowl)
1 1/2 cups cabbage, shredded
1 beef bouillon (cube or tsp.)
1 chicken bouillon (cube or tsp.)

Wash meat under hot water, then add to 2 quarts boiling water. Cook about 1 hour, skimming off top when necessary. Test for doneness. Cook longer if necessary according to cut of meat used. Put in rest of ingredients and simmer for 15 minutes. Do not overcook vegetables. Put in fresh serving of parsley, chopped, just before serving. Serve with boiled parsley potatoes, lok sauce and meat dumplings.

LOK SAUCE (ONION SAUCE)

1 tbsp. butter
1 tbsp. all-purpose flour
1 onion, grated

meat broth
1 tbsp. sugar
1 tbsp. vinegar

Melt butter in pan. Saute onion until transparent. Sprinkle in flour, making sure there are no lumps. Slowly add broth. Add vinegar and sugar. Add more broth to desired consistency. Serve on meat and potatoes.

SODDBOLLER (MEAT DUMPLINGS)

1/2 lb. ground round
1 tsp. salt
1 medium onion
1 tbsp. or more potato flour (or Argo cornstarch)
1 tbsp. all-purpose flour
1 1/4 cups milk (can be mixed with cream or canned milk)
dash nutmeg
dash white pepper

If using hand grinder, grind meat 5 times with 1 tsp. salt. Add chopped onion for second 5 times. If using a food processor, grind for 30 seconds with salt and 30 seconds with onion. Grind again with all ingredients except milk and nutmeg, which is added last. Make into small balls and simmer in soup broth for 5 minutes. Let stand in broth. Add to Kjot Suppe just before serving.

GLUGG

Bottle (Fifth) each of Rum, Port and Sherry
1 cup raisins, seedless
1 cup whole almonds, blanched *
12 cloves
15 cardomoner seeds **
orange rind (scrape off white part), grated finely

* soak in hot water 5 minutes, till jacket is loose. Press and nut will pop
from skin.

** remove seeds from shell and discard shell.

Combine everything in large pot. Bring entire mixture almost to the boiling
point. Put match to Glugg and allow to burn 30 to 60 seconds while
sprinkling about one heaping tbsp. of sugar over the flame. This will
caramelize the sugar and add a richer taste. If possible, let stand at least 1
week. When serving, heat up enough for the number of guests. Serve in a
mug with a spoon to eat the fruit. Goes great with crisp Christmas cookies.

From Mrs. Shirley Anschutz of Staunton, Illinois:

A Swedish great-grandfather of mine came through Ellis Island during the great immigration. His name was Christian Person (sometimes spelled Parson or Parsons.) His destination was Afton, Minnesota, on the St. Croix River - near St. Paul, one of the most beautiful spots on earth even now. *His son-in-law, my Swede grandfather, also came through Ellis Island at a different time, but with the same destination. His name was Charles Swanson - when he left Sweden for the U.S. it was Karl Nelson, but his father's name was Swan Nelson, so he used the "Swan" and added "son" for a surname! Done often in those days, I'm told. Grandpa Charley, as we called him, learned to cook simple things as his wife died young and he was left with small children to care for, my mother, Gladys, being one of them. This was how he wrote down the recipe for "Swedish Rice." It is made in a casserole in the oven with just raw rice, sugar, and milk and must stand to cool a while before serving, or it is very "soupy." An absolutely delicious dessert.*

CHARLIE SWANSON'S SWEDISH RICE

4 cups milk (can use more - up to 6 cups!)
1/2 cup uncooked rice
1/2 cup sugar

This is baked in a moderate oven for 1 1/2 hours in a pan or casserole. So easy and sweet and delicious you won't believe it. Let it set a while until just warm after baking or else it will be too "soupy". Serve in dessert dishes. Use uncooked rice. Sprinkle cinnamon on top and bake it. Don't stir while it is baking.

From Nancy L. Blomquist of Castine, Maine:

My husband's heritage is Swedish (I'm a "damn Yankee"-mixed breed, as they say). His father, Axel Fritzhof Blomquist, came to the United States in 1906 at the age of eighteen and settled in Gardner, Massachusetts, where he met and married my husband's mother, Mamie L. Stenquist, whose parents were both born in Sweden as well; he was Axel Robert Stenquist and she was Christine Louise Erickson.

SWEDISH ROT MUS

2 lbs. spare ribs (regular, cracked twice)
1 orange turnip (rutabaga), peeled and cut into 4 pieces
4 medium potatoes

In a large pot, cover the spare ribs and turnip with water and simmer 45 minutes. Add potatoes and cook another 30 minutes until the potatoes are soft. Pour off the water; put spare ribs on a serving dish; mash the turnip and potato together. Add butter, and salt and pepper to taste. Preparation time: 1 1/4 hours. Serves 4-6.

We would fry any leftover turnip/potatoes. Umm - good!

From Margaret Carlson of Amery, Wisconsin:

My mother, Ingrid Sandberg Carlson, came to the United States in 1910 at the age of nineteen. She came all alone and never made a return trip to Sweden. She went to Minneapolis, Minnesota, where she had two uncles living. She worked as a maid until her marriage in 1916 and a move to a farm in Wisconsin.

My mother was an excellent cook, but to our loss there were very few recipes -- cook and season as she went along. This simple cake was stirred up and baked on short notice when company "dropped in" - no telephoning ahead but what enjoyable times those visits were!

SOUR CREAM CAKES

2 eggs
sour cream
1 1/2 cups all-purpose flour
1 cup sugar

1/4 tsp. soda
1 tsp. baking powder
1 tsp. vanilla
whipping cream

Break the 2 eggs in a 1 cup measure; fill up with sour cream. Beat well. Sift the dry ingredients and add to egg and cream mixture. Add the vanilla. Pour into an 8" square pan; greased and floured lightly. Bake 30 minutes in 325° oven. Cool and cover with whipped cream. Serves 9.

From Ruby Ebert Page of Tallahassee, Florida:

Here is a favorite recipe of my family from my mother's time, which I remember from childhood.

Adina(h) Elvira Dahlberg Ebert, my mother, left Helsingborg, Sweden, in February 1904 according to the parish records in Viken, just north of Helsingborg, where she was born. This was one of my favorite recipes as she made it with tender loving care when we were ill. The tradition continued with my children and now with their children. Just recently, my two-year old granddaughter had a bad allergy and asked for that good, homemade potato soup to make her feel better. It does make one feel better through nutrition and love.

ADINAH'S POTATO SOUP

4-5 medium-size potatoes
1 medium-size onion
1 1/2 cups milk
 (or 3/4 cup evaporated milk)
1 1/2 tbsp. butter
salt & pepper, to taste

Pare and chip potatoes. Into 1 quart salted water add potatoes and chipped onion. Boil until tender. Reduce to simmer. Remove 2 cups of the water and add whole milk (or remove 1 cup of water and add the evaporated milk). Add butter and pepper.

From Mrs. Dorothy Snow of Huntington Valley, Pennsylvania:

This recipe is from my grandmother, Evelyn Jacobson Lundmark. She was born in Goteborg, Sweden, in 1869. Many in the family still make and enjoy Pult.

PULT - PALT - SIMLE

10-12 potatoes, peeled
1 cup all-purpose flour
1/2 lb. salt pork, lean
2 tsp. baking powder
2 tsp. salt
3 cups graham flour

Grind potatoes, sprinkle with graham flour to prevent darkening. Dice lean pork, cut fat into strips and grind along with potatoes. Add baking powder and salt. Add regular flour until you can make a ball. Make a dent in center for 1\2 tsp. or so of diced, lean pork. Form a ball. Carefully drop into boiling salted water. Boil 1 hour. Serve with butter and some broth. For another meal, slice and fry. Serve with butter and chili sauce. Yields 12 dumplings, 3" diameter.

From Betty Young of Alamosa, Colorado:

Here is a recipe my father, Berndt Perssou, brought from Sweden. Our family has used it for many years, especially for Christmas Eve smorgasbord.

PICKLED SALT HERRING (INLAGD SILL)

1 large salt herring

Dressing

1/2 cup white vinegar
1 tsp. water
1/4 cup sugar
2 tsp. chopped onion
4 white peppercorns, crushed
4 whole allspice, crushed

Garnish

Sliced onion and dill

Clean fish, removing head and soak overnight in cold water. Bone and fillet. Cut in small slices then slide spatula under slices and arrange like whole fish in glass plate. Mix ingredients for dressing and pour over. Garnish with onion rings and dill weed. Leave 2-3 hours in refrigerator before serving.

MAJOR ETHNIC ORGANIZATIONS

Alliance of Poles in America, 6966 Broadway, Cleveland, OH 44105

The American Historical Society of Germans From Russia, 631 D Street, Lincoln, NE 68502

American Committee on Italian Migration, 352 West 44 Street, New York, NY 10036

American Hungarian Federation, 2631 Copley Road, Akron, OH 44321

American Latvian Association in the United States, P.O. Box 4578 Rockville, MD 20850

American Scandinavian Foundation, 725 Park Avenue, New York, NY 10021

American Slovenian Catholic Union, 2439 Glenwood Avenue, Joliet, IL 60435

American Scottish Foundation, Inc. P.O. Box 537, Lenox Hill Station, New York, NY 10021

American-Swiss Association, Inc. 10 East 53 Street, 32 Floor, New York, NY 10022

Ancient Order of Hibernians in America, 31 Logan Street, Auburn, NY 13021

Austrian American Federation, 31 East 69 Street, New York, NY 10012

B'nai B'rith, 1640 Rhode Island Avenue, N. W., Washington, DC 20036

Baltic Women's Council, 414 Abington Place, East Meadow, NY 11554

British Heritage Society, 7235 Pine Grove, Houston, TX 77092

Catholic Workman - Katolicky Delnik - Post Office Box 47, New Prague, MN 56071

Congress of Russian Americans, P.O. Box 818, Nyack, NY 10960

Croatian Catholic Union of the U.S.A., One West Old Ridge Road, Hobart, IN 46342

Croatian Fraternal Union of America, 100 Delaney Drive, Pittsburgh, PA 15235

Czechoslovak Society of America, 2701 South Harlem Avenue, Berwyn, IL 60402

Danish Brotherhood in America, 3717 Harney Street, Omaha, NE 68131

Dutch Amer. Hist. Com., Calvin Theol. Sem., 3233 Burton Street, S.E. Grand Rapids, MI 49546

Federation of Turkish American Societies, 821 United Nations Plaza, New York, NY 10017

First Cath. Slovak Un. of the U. S. and Canada, 6611 Rockside Road, Independence, OH 44131

Franco-American Historical Society, One Social Street, Post Office Box F, Woonsocket, RI 02895

German-American National Congress, 4740 North Western Avenue, 2 Floor, Chicago, IL 60625

The German Society of the City of New York, 6 East 87 Street, New York, NY 10128

Germans from Russia Heritage Society, 1008 East Central Avenue, Bismark, ND 58501

Hebrew Immigrant Aid Society (HIAS), 333 Seventh Avenue, New York, NY 10001

Hungarian Reformed Fed. America, 2001 Massachusetts Avenue, N.W., Washington, DC 20036

Italian Catholic Federation Central Council, 1801 Van Ness Avenue, San Francisco, CA 94109

Lithuanian Roman Catholic Federation of America, 4545 West 63 Street, Chicago, IL 60629

National Council of Jewish Women, 53 West 23 Street, New York, NY 10010

National Slavic Convention, 16 South Patterson Park Avenue, Baltimore, MD 21231

National Slavic Society of the United States, 2325 East Carson Street, Pittsburgh, PA 15203

The Netherland Club of New York, 10 Rockefeller Plaza, New York, NY 10020

Netherlands-America Community Association, One Rockefeller Plaza, New York, NY 10020

Order Of Ahepa, 1909 Q Street, N.W., Washington, DC 20009

Orders Sons of Italy in America, 219 E Street, N.E., Washington, DC 20002

Polish American Congress, 5711 North Milwaukee Avenue, Chicago, IL 60646

Polish Falcons of America, 97 South 18 Street, Pittsburgh, PA 15203

Polish National Alliance, 6100 North Cicero, Chicago, IL 60646

Polish National Union of America, 1002 Pittman Avenue, Scranton, PA 18505

Polish Roman Catholic Union of America, 984 Milwaukee Avenue, Chicago, IL 60622

Polish Union of America, Box 79, 761 Filmore Avenue, Buffalo, NY 14212

Providence Assn. of Ukranian Cath.in Amer., 817 N. Franklin St., Philadelphia, PA 19123

Russian Brotherhood Org. of the U.S.A., 1733 Spring Garden Street, Philadelphia, PA 19130

Selfreliance Association of American Ukranians, 98 Second Avenue, New York, NY 10003

Serbian National Defense Council, 5782 North Alston, Chicago, Il 60646

Slovak-American National Council, P.O. Box 264, Oakton, VA 22124

Slovene National Benefit Society, 166 Shore Drive, Burr Ridge, IL 60521

Society Farsarotul, Post Office Box 753, Trumbell, CT 06611

Sons of Norway, 1455 West Lake Street, Minneapolis, MN 55408

St. Davids Society of the State of New York, 71 West 23 Street, New York, NY 10010

Supreme Lodge of the Danish Sisterhood in Amer., 4312 N. Keeler Ave., Chicago, IL 60641

Ukranian National Association, 30 Montgomery Street, Jersey City, NJ 07302

Ukranian National Womens League of America, 108 Second Avenue, New York, NY 10003

Union and League of Romanian Soc. of Amer., 23203 Lorain Rd., North Olmsted, OH 44070

United Jewish Appeal, 99 Park Avenue, New York, NY 10016

United Swedish Societies, 20 Bristol Avenue, Staten Island, NY 10301

William Penn Association (Hungrian), 709 Brighton Road, Pittsburgh, PA 15233

IMMIGRANT PORTRAITS

The following photographs were discovered in 1986 in a church in Alfreton, England, the birthplace of Robert Watchorn, commissioner of immigration at Ellis Island from 1905 to 1909.

SHEPHERD
DESTINATION: WYOMING

IRISH SERVANT
DESTINATION: NEW YORK CITY

ITALIAN DOMESTIC
DESTINATION: LOWELL,
MASSACHUSETTS

RUSSIAN CATTLE DEALER
DESTINATION: FARGO,
NORTH DAKOTA

HUNGARIAN WIFE
DESTINATION: CHICAGO

ITALIAN LABORER
DESTINATION: ST. LOUIS

SWEDISH FARMER
DESTINATION: SOUTH DAKOTA

RUSSIAN WIDOW
DESTINATION: LANCASTER,
PENNSYLVANIA

HUNGARIAN FARMER
DESTINATION: OHIO

CHILD DETAINED
SICKNESSS IN FAMILY

HUNGARIAN SERVANT
DESTINATION: TRENTON,
NEW JERSEY

RUSSIAN SERVANT
DESTINATION: SALEM,
MASSACHUSETTS

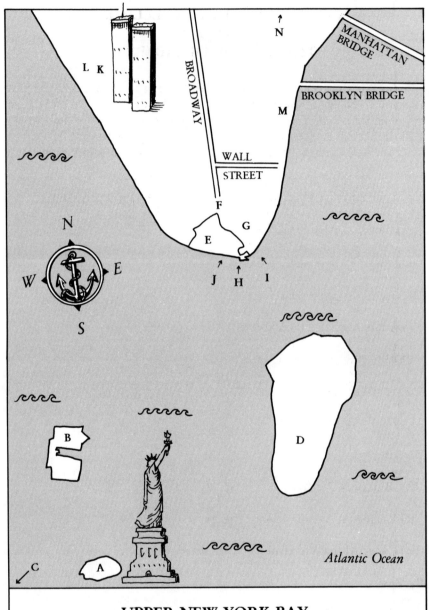

UPPER NEW YORK BAY

A. LIBERTY ISLAND
B. ELLIS ISLAND
C. LIBERTY STATE PARK
D. GOVERNORS ISLAND
E. CASTLE CLINTON, BATTERY PARK
F. BOWLING GREEN SUBWAY STOP
G. WHITEHALL SUBWAY STOP

H. SOUTH FERRY SUBWAY STOP
I. STATEN ISLAND FERRY
J. THE PETREL
K. WORLD TRADE CENTER
L. WORLD FINANCIAL CENTER
M. SOUTH STREET SEAPORT
N. THE TENEMENT MUSEUM

PLANNING YOUR TRIP TO ELLIS ISLAND
AND
THE STATUE OF LIBERTY

Both Ellis Island and the Statue of Liberty are open every day of the year except Christmas. Admission to both is free. However, there is a charge to get to either island. You must take a Circle Line ferry from either Battery Park in Manhattan or from Liberty State Park in New Jersey. Boats leave approximately every hour. For up-to-date information on schedules and fares call:

TO GET TO ELLIS ISLAND AND THE STATUE OF LIBERTY:

From Battery Park (Manhattan):

212-269-5755 - fares and schedule

212-363-3200 - general information

From Liberty State Park (New Jersey):

201-435-9499 - fares and schedules

201-915-3401 - general park information

TO GET TO BATTERY PARK AND SOUTH FERRY:

By Subway:

IRT Broadway 7th Avenue LOCAL (#1 or #9) to South Ferry
or
IRT Lexington Avenue Express (#4) to Bowling Green
or
BMT LOCAL to Whitehall (N or R)

By Bus:

Broadway Bus (#M-6) to last stop: South Ferry

By Taxi:

South Ferry or Battery Park

Parking: Very limited parking Monday to Friday. Parking is available Saturdays, Sundays and Holidays.

FOR FURTHER INFORMATION:

For further information about The Statue of Liberty or Ellis Island, you can call the National Park Service at 212-363-7620 or write to The Statue Of Liberty National Monument, Liberty Island, New York, New York 10004. The N.P.S. also maintains other sites in Manhattan, including Federal Hall and The Theodore Roosevelt Birthplace. For information on those additional sites, call 212-825-6888 or write to Federal Hall National Memorial at 26 Wall Street, New York, New York 10005.

TICKETS:

Tickets for The Statue of Liberty and Ellis Island ferries leaving from Manhattan are purchased at Castle Clinton (Castle Garden), in the middle of Battery Park. This historic structure dating back to the War of 1812 has had a rich and diversified history. Built as a fort in the water to repel the British in 1814, it was later joined to the mainland. A roof was added and it became a popular entertainment center. It is here that Jenny Lind, the famous Swedish Nightingale, made her American debut on September 11, 1850, before an audience of 10,000 fans. From 1855 until 1890, it was the major port of entry for immigrants to the United States. It is here that many Germans and many of the Irish escaping the Potato Famine entered the United States. As the direct predecessor to Ellis Island, it deserves our attention. In the early part of this century it became the New York Aquarium. Now it is restored to its role as a fort. While waiting to get your tickets for the ferry, I recommend you spend a few minutes to look at the exhibits lining the walls. They will familiarize you with the history of the harbor and set the stage for your trip to Ellis. The ferries leave nearby, where once the immigrants were put on barges for the trip to Ellis and their inspection.

Tickets for ferries from New Jersey are purchased at Liberty State Park in Jersey City, New Jersey, Exit 14-B on the New Jersey Turnpike.

TOURS:

Reservations for tours of the Statue of Liberty and Ellis Island must be made at least two weeks in advance. Call 212-363-7620. Reservations should be made as early as possible.

ACCOMMODATIONS:

For information on other places of interest and hotels contact:

The New York Convention and Visitors' Bureau
2 Columbus Circle
New York, New York 10019
212-397-8222
Publishes a list of hotels, sites, restaurants etc.

State Of New York Division Of Tourism
N. Y. State Department Of Economic Development
1 Commerce Plaza
Albany, New York 12245

For general New York State Tourism information, dial toll-free 800-CALL-NYS (800-225-5697) throughout the continental U. S., from everywhere else, 518-474-4116.

ADDITIONAL:

While in lower Manhattan you may also want to visit other historical sites or points of interest. For a definitive New York experience, the *Staten Island Ferry* leaves frequently just outside Battery Park. A round-trip takes about one hour.

Casting off from Battery Park is *The Petrel*, a 70-foot teak and mahogany sailing yawl, a favorite of the late President Kennedy. In season (May-October) it features public and private excursions, including a sunset cruise (212-825-1976).

The World Trade Center Observation Deck (212-435-7397, South Tower) and the *World Financial Center* (212-945-0505) are located nearby. Half-price theater tickets, for the day of performance, can be purchased in the mezzanine of Two World Trade Center at *TKTS*.

Across town, on the East River, is the *South Street Seaport*. This historic area includes restorations of buildings and ships, as well as many shops and restaurants. (Visitors' Center: 212-748-8600, Ext. 659. General information and museum: 212-748-8600.

To continue your Ellis Island experience, you may want to visit *The Tenement Museum* at 97 Orchard Street (212-431-0233) on the Lower East Side.

ELLIS ISLAND TODAY

With the passage of the 1924 quota laws, Ellis Island's chapter as the main immigration inspection center in the U. S. ended. With strict limited quotas, most of the inspection was done prior to boarding a ship in the country of departure. Immigrants were brought to Ellis Island only under special circumstances.

During World War II, the Coast Guard used the facilities and it became a hospital for wounded soldiers. Most of the immigrants housed there were those about to be deported: illegal aliens or those that had violated the terms of entry.

By 1954 it made no sense to maintain the huge facilities and the Federal Government moved off. It took no time for the vandals to move on. Just about everything of value disappeared, including most of the copper roofing, legal desks and other irreplaceable artifacts. The windows were broken; birds and nature moved in. In winter, the freezing temperature burst the pipes; ceilings and floors crumbled. It sat there for fifteen years. As the immigrants became further assimilated, had children, and enjoyed the rewards of their journey, their stepping stone deteriorated rapidly. For many who came through Ellis, it was a place to forget. The climate of the country did not celebrate ethnic identity as it does now. Ellis was put on the auction block for prospective development.

In 1965, President Lyndon Johnson transferred jurisdiction to the National Park Service and it became part of The Statue of Liberty National Monument. Then, in 1976, parts of the island were open for limited visitation. For six months of the year, tour guides led groups through the eerie ruins. Most of the island was hard-hat area and the visitors had to be closely watched. Public interest increased and various groups concerned with the future of Ellis Island were formed. With political pressure and the restoration of the Statue of Liberty about to begin, it was decided to restore the island and the public was invited to become part of this unique restoration.

In 1984 the island closed once again and restoration began. Costing over 150 million dollars, it represents the largest restoration project undertaken in American history.

Today, the peeling paint and crumbling walls are gone. The steel and glass canopy, torn down in 1933, has been replaced. Reproductions of legal desks stand in the Registry Room. The original benches have been put back, providing a good resting spot to contemplate the saga of these "huddled masses, yearning to breathe free."

MAP OF ELLIS ISLAND

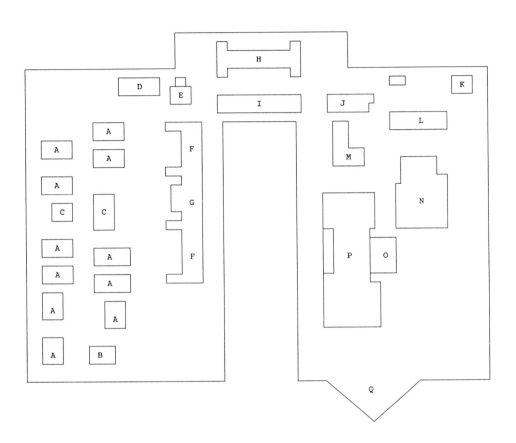

A CONTAGIOUS DISEASE WARDS
B STAFF HOUSE
C ADMINISTRATION
  BUILDING
D RECREATION HALL
E LAUNDRY BUILDING
F HOSPITAL
G ADMINISTRATION
  BUILDING
H NEW IMMIGRATION
  BUILDING
I NEW FERRY BUILDING

J BAKERY AND CARPENTRY
  SHOP
K GREENHOUSE
L MAIN POWERHOUSE
M KITCHEN AND LAUNDRY
  BUILDING
N BAGGAGE AND DORMITORY
  BUILDING
O RAILROAD TICKET OFFICE
P MAIN BUILDING
Q WALL OF HONOR

FIRST FLOOR

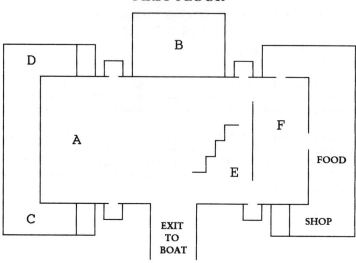

SECOND FLOOR

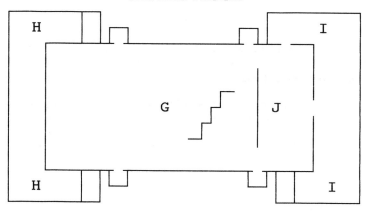

THIRD FLOOR

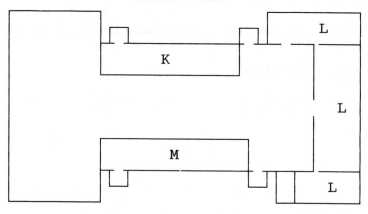

ELLIS ISLAND MUSEUM DIRECTORY

FIRST FLOOR:

A THE INFORMATION DESK, in the former baggage room, provides information on the showing of a half-hour film "Island Of Hope/Island Of Tears", shown in two theaters and schedules of return trips to Manhattan and New Jersey.

B THE PEOPLING OF AMERICA, located in the old railroad ticket office, places the Ellis Island immigration era into the context of 400 years of immigration history. Exhibits include "Where We Are: Ethnic Groups in America", "Millions On The Move: Worldwide Migrations", The World Tree: Ethnic Americanisms" and "Today's Immigrants."

C CHANGING EXHIBITS

D AMERICA'S FAMILY ALBUM, a video exhibit of photos submitted by Americans specifically for this exhibit.

E WALL OF HONOR, computer terminals to locate seawall panels containing names of contributors to the restoration of Ellis Island.

F THEATER 1

SECOND FLOOR:

G REGISTRY ROOM, the historic Great Hall.

H THROUGH AMERICA'S GATE, a 14-room exhibit area detailing the Ellis Island immigration process through photos, artifacts and personal papers.

I PEAK IMMIGRATION YEARS, tells the larger story of immigrants during the great migration to the U.S. regardless of the port of entry.

J THEATER 2

THIRD FLOOR:

K DORMITORY ROOM, circa 1908

L ELLIS ISLAND GALLERIES, including "Treasures From Home", "Ellis Island Chronicles", "Silent Voices, and "Restoring A Landmark".

M CHANGING EXHIBITS

The museum also houses an oral history studio containing a large collection of taped reminiscences of Ellis Island Immigrants and former immigration employees.

Also of interest is The Ellis Island Learning Center, where the drama of the immigrant experience comes alive on a 16-screem Videowall. Here today's video and computer technology unite to provide a memorable interactive learing experience.

To make an appointment to visit the Learning Center or the oral history studio, write to: Museum Services Division, The Statue Of Liberty National Monument, Liberty Island, New York 10004

TIPS ON TRACING YOUR FAMILY ROOTS

Part detective work and part history lesson, tracing your family roots can be a most rewarding and enjoyable endeavor. By tracing your roots now, you can assure future generations this link with their past. It can also reinforce a sense of family tradition and history. By enlisting younger family members, you can also provide valuable lessons in history and develop research skills. Older family members are a great source of family history. Talking with them and showing an interest in their lives are wonderful ways to bridge generation gaps.

The following are some tips on tracing your family roots:

- Start with a family tree and fill in as much information as you can. From there, interview family members who might know missing information.

- Find out who has old family photos. Make enlarged photocopies so you can label unknown ancestors. It is easier to get a "feel" for your ancestors if you can put a face to the name. Be sure to label the backs of photos, both old and new, with names, dates and locations.

- Start by interviewing older family members. A tape recorder will be helpful. When taking notes, be as complete as possible. Notes that seem clear now may be confusing a month later. Old photos can provide a launching off point to help in remembering family history.

- The family Bible, photo album, scrap book or old letters may contain valuable information. Also check: birth, marriage, death certificates and military records.

- Visit the graves of ancestors to obtain or check information.

- Remember, a family history is more than just data. By writing a brief history of notable events or people, you can add so much more to your project.

ANCESTRY OF

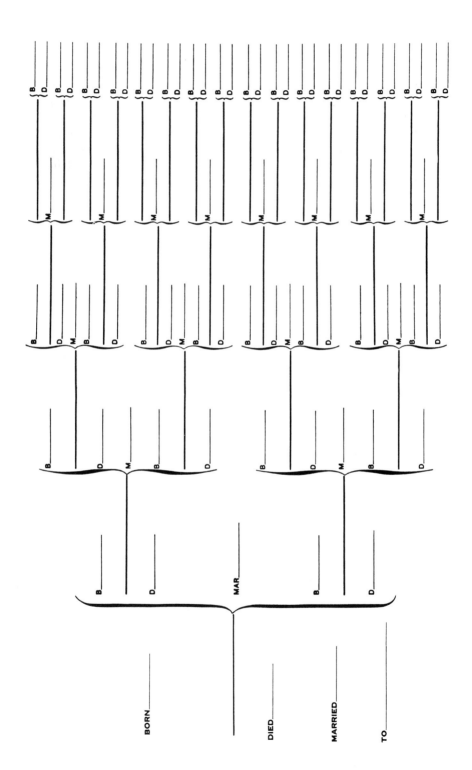

BORN

DIED

MARRIED

TO

IMMIGRANT ANCESTOR INFORMATION

NAME:_____ RELATIONSHIP: _____

PLACE OF BIRTH:_____ DATE OF BIRTH:_____

STEAMSHIP NAME:_____

PORT OF DEPARTURE:_____

DATE OF DEPARTURE:_____

PORT OF ARRIVAL:_____

DATE OF ARRIVAL:_____

COMMENTS:_____

NAME:_____ RELATIONSHIP: _____

PLACE OF BIRTH:_____ DATE OF BIRTH:_____

STEAMSHIP NAME:_____

PORT OF DEPARTURE:_____

DATE OF DEPARTURE:_____

PORT OF ARRIVAL:_____

DATE OF ARRIVAL:_____

COMMENTS:_____

NAME:_____ RELATIONSHIP: _____

PLACE OF BIRTH:_____ DATE OF BIRTH:_____

STEAMSHIP NAME:_____

PORT OF DEPARTURE:_____

DATE OF DEPARTURE:_____

PORT OF ARRIVAL:_____

DATE OF ARRIVAL:_____

COMMENTS:_____

NAME:_____ RELATIONSHIP: _____

PLACE OF BIRTH:_____ DATE OF BIRTH:_____

STEAMSHIP NAME:_____

PORT OF DEPARTURE:_____

DATE OF DEPARTURE:_____

PORT OF ARRIVAL:_____

DATE OF ARRIVAL:_____

COMMENTS:_____

GENEALOGICAL SEARCH INFORMATION

GOVERNMENT SOURCES

The Statue of Liberty National Monument does not have the facilities available to conduct genealogical searches.

Contact the following organizations for assistance:

National Archives and Records Service
Research Services Branch
General Services Administration
Washington, D.C. 20408

Historical Reference Library and Reading Room Section
Immigration and Naturalization Services
425 I Street N. W., Room 1100 A
Washington, D. C. 20536

National Archives-Northeast Region
201 Varick Street
New York, New York 10014

Superintendent Of Documents
U.S. Government Printing Office
Washington, D. C. 20402

The Smithsonian Institution publishes a booklet called "Family Folklore - Interviewing Guide And Questionnaire." Write to the above address for information.

PRIVATE RESOURCES

The following are publishers, bookstores and search service companies. Many have free catalogues upon request:

Ancestry Incorporated
P. O. Box 476
Salt Lake city, Utah 84110

Genealogical Publishing Company
1001 North Calvert Street
Baltimore, Maryland 21202

Goodspeed's Bookshop
7 Beacon Street
Boston, Massachusetts 02108

Southern Historical Press
P. O. Box 738
Easley, South Carolina 29641

Genealogy Unlimited
Post Office Box 537
Orem, Utah 84059

Lineages, Inc.
350 South 400 East #202
Salt Lake City, Utah 84111

Light Impressions (Archival supplies)
439 Monroe Avenue
Rochester, New York 14607-3717

In addition, The Church Of Jesus Christ Latter-Day Saints has the largest collection of genealogical information in the world. Contact:

Family History Library
35 N. West Temple Street
Salt Lake City, Utah 84150

ORAL HISTORY PROJECT

The Statue of Liberty National Monument is interested in hearing from former immigrants processed at Ellis Island and former Ellis Island employees. They have issued the following guidelines for those interested in being part of this important project. If you are interested in taking part, please answer the following questions and return them to the address below. It is understood that not everyone will be able to answer every question. Please do not leave your reply at the Museum. Only adequately completed forms mailed to the Statute will be considered for the Oral History Project.

Each adequately completed form will be reviewed to determine eligibility for the Project and each applicant will be contacted with the decision to keep the form on file for the present or to proceed with a scheduled interview.

All forms and interviews will become part of the museum's extensive Oral History Collection for use by researchers, historians, and interested members of the public and stored at the Ellis Island Immigration Museum. All completed forms will be kept on file. All interviews are available as printed transcripts and audio cassette tapes.

Because of the enormous response to the Project they ask that you be patient for a response after you have mailed the completed form.

On a separate piece(s) of paper, answer the following questions and return them to the following address:

Oral History Project
Museum Services Division
Statue Of Liberty National Monument
Liberty Island
New York, New York 10004.

- Name:

- Country Of Origin:

- Date Of Birth:

- Reasons For Immigrating:

- Family Members Who Accompanied You On The Voyage:

- Port Of Departure:

- Date Or Season Of Departure:

- Name Of Ship:

- Any Details Of Voyage:

- Any Memories Of Seeing The Statue Of Liberty And New York For The First Time:

- Age Upon Arrival At Ellis Island:

- Any Memories Of Facilities And Processing At Ellis Island (i.e. Medical Exams, Legal Problems, Baggage Claims, Money Exchange, Food, etc):

- Were You Detained Overnight Or Longer At Ellis Island ? Why ?

- Where Did You Go After You Left Ellis Island ?

- Any Other Details, Anecdotes, Stories, Memories You Would Like To Share About Your Immigration Experience And Ellis Island:

TIPS ON PRESERVING A FAMILY RECIPE

By sharing these recipes and stories, the contributors to this book have clearly shown the importance and rewards of preserving our culinary past.

Experienced cooks in everyday cooking frequently do so without measuring utensils or strict adherence to recipes. The process to them is so easy and familiar that it's hard to realize that they at one time were novices. The preparation of family meals was (and hopefully still is) considered part of a child's education and family duties. They learned to cook standing at their mother's side as she had done in her youth. Now, life in the late twentieth century seems to provide fewer of these opportunities and it is up to us to insure that favorite old family recipes and traditions are not lost to future generations. The following are some suggestions in gleaning a treasured recipe:

- Discuss your goal with the family cook.

- On paper, list the ingredients and their quantities. What measuring utensils will be needed? What size pots and pans are required? Approximately how long will the recipe take to prepare? How long will it take to cook or bake? Are there preparations that have to be done beforehand? What traditions or serving suggestions accompany the dish? What family stories? What changes have been made over the years ?

- Take notes as you discuss the recipe.

- Participate in the preparation. If possible, prepare the recipe twice, once as an observer and note-taker and the second time as the cook, making corrections and additions as you proceed.

- Before the cook adds "a pinch of this" or "handful of that," intercept into a measuring utensil.

- Are there any preparation techniques that are unique or traditional in its preparation?

- If possible, use a tape recorder for complete accuracy. A camera could be helpful to photograph the process in various stages and the finished dish.

- Try out the recipe and write it down before entering it in this book. Remember, you are saving this part of your history for future generations and including personal details will greatly enhance the enjoyment of the recipe.

TREASURED FAMILY RECIPE

RECIPE TITLE: _____

RECIPE OF: _____

ARRIVED IN AMERICA FROM: _____ *DATE:* _____

INGREDIENTS:

_____   _____

_____   _____

_____   _____

_____   _____

INSTRUCTIONS: _____

_____

_____

_____

_____

COMMENTS: _____

_____

_____

_____

DATE RECORDED: _____ *BY:* _____

TREASURED FAMILY RECIPE

RECIPE TITLE: _____

RECIPE OF: _____

ARRIVED IN AMERICA FROM: _____ DATE: _____

INGREDIENTS:

_____   _____

_____   _____

_____   _____

_____   _____

INSTRUCTIONS: _____

_____

_____

_____

_____

COMMENTS: _____

_____

_____

_____

DATE RECORDED: _____   BY: _____

TREASURED FAMILY RECIPE

RECIPE TITLE: _____

RECIPE OF: _____

ARRIVED IN AMERICA FROM: _____ *DATE:* _____

INGREDIENTS:

_____   _____

_____   _____

_____   _____

_____   _____

INSTRUCTIONS: _____

_____

_____

_____

_____

COMMENTS: _____

_____

_____

_____

DATE RECORDED: _____ *BY:* _____

HOW TO CONTRIBUTE TO THE PRESERVATION
OF ELLIS ISLAND

THE AMERICAN IMMIGRANT WALL OF HONOR

The Statue of Liberty-Ellis Island Foundation, Inc. is accepting names to be included on The American Immigrant Wall Of Honor.

This monument to the immigrants who came to America, regardless of when they came or where they entered, is a permanent exhibit of individual or family names, engraved for posterity at Ellis Island. The names of over 420,000 individuals and families are inscribed on this tribute to our nation's immigrant heritage. You can have your family name included on the wall by filling out a Registration Form and contributing $100.00.

Donors will receive an 8 1/2" x 11" certificate, personalized with the name and country of the ancestor you choose to honor.

At Ellis Island you can locate the section of the wall bearing your family name by using a computer terminal located on the first floor of the Ellis Island Museum.

After the closing date for accepting new names you can still donate to a general fund for the restoration of Ellis Island.

For more information and a registration form, contact:

Ellis Campaign
P.O. Box Ellis
New York, New York 10163

or call: 212-883-1986

FOR FURTHER READING

Benton, Barbara. *Ellis Island: A Pictorial History.* New York: Facts On File Publications, 1985.

Corsi, Edward. *In the Shadow of Liberty: The Chronicle of Ellis Island.* New York: Macmillan, 1935.

Heaps, Willard. *The Story of Ellis Island.* New York: Seabury, 1967.

Jonas, Susan., ed. *Ellis Island: Echoes from a Nation's Past.* New York: Aperture Foundation, Inc., 1989.

Novotny, Ann. *Strangers at The Door: Ellis Island, Castle Garden and the Great Migration to America.* Connecticut: The Chatham Press, Inc., 1971.

Pitkin, Thomas. *Keepers of the Gate, A History of Ellis Island.* New York University Press, 1975.

Reeves, Pamela. *Ellis Island: Gateway to the American Dream.* New York: Dorset Press, 1991.

Tifft, Wilton. *Ellis Island.* Chicago: Contemporary Books, Inc., 1990.

ABOUT THE AUTHOR

In 1885, arriving in Lawrence, Massachusetts, from Canada, was a family of eleven, the Blanchettes: Georgiana, Albert, Eugenie (my grandmother), Alphonse, Wilfred, Julia, George, Arthur, Adelard, Frederic and their father, Nazaire, my great-grandfather. Their mother, Marcelline, had died a year earlier after complications from childbirth.

Life on the northern farms was surely a most difficult life. A family historian wrote of the Blanchettes:

> *"When the day's temperature rose above freezing and the night saw it dip below once again, almost all activity in Warwick turned to collecting and boiling off sap from the Maple tree. It was very much a family activity as the boys gathered the sap and kept the sugaring shed stocked with firewood. Nazaire would supervise the boiling of the sap, watching closely for the instant the sap became syrup. Once it reached the proper consistency, the hot syrup would then be poured off and Marcelline and the girls would take over. They would carefully pour the hot syrup into molds of various shapes where it would cool, harden and be used for candy or sugar. Some syrup would also be stored in containers for later use. Although hard work, sugaring brought many rewards to the family, especially to the children; syrup poured over the snow and later eaten taffy-like was a great treat.... Winter cold, however, did help provide better storage of food. Nazaire would use wooden barrels as refrigerators by freezing a thick layer of ice in each end and cutting a hatch door in the side of the barrel. He would place whole, stuffed frozen chickens or chunks of pork or beef inside where they would be well-preserved out in the cold winter air."*

Lawrence at that time was a thriving mill town. Down river (the Merrimac) from Lowell, (now a National Park Service site important for its mills and innovative worker housing), it had an extensive network of canals which was attractive to the mill owners as a source of power. To Canadian farmers, living on remote farms, it promised opportunity and work, no doubt the motivating influence to relocate such large families. Lawrence was surely the destination for many immigrants passing through Ellis Island. It was also the site of the Bread And Roses Strike Of 1912, an important chapter in the story of workers' rights.

The Bernardins, Charles and Victoire, also from Canada, had arrived in Lawrence a few years earlier with their many children: Marie, Rosilda, Charles, Emma, Celanire, Catherine, Victorine, Magloire (my grandfather), Angelique, Eugene and Abelard. They too were seeking a better life and the family shortly went into the butter and egg delivery business.

While on his butter and egg route, Charles Bernardin Jr. met Georgiana Blanchette and they married. Her sister, Eugenie, met his brother, Maglorie, and they too married, and in 1948 became my grandparents.

The following two recipes were brought down from Canada by my great-grandparents. My New York Irish mother wasted no time in learning to cook them.

CRETONS

3 lbs. fresh pork, ground, not too lean
4 medium or two large onions, chopped fine
salt and pepper
bay leaf

Cover meat and onions with water and cook very slowly in an iron skillet without a cover for 3-4 hours.

For the last hour of cooking add:

1/2 tsp. ground cloves
1/2 tsp. cinnamon

Stir often to prevent burning. Spoon into jelly jars, do not remove fat. This was served as a spread on crackers, as a side dish for Boston Baked Beans, but, in my opinion, best on homemade toast and jelly for breakfast.

My Aunt Edmee often told the following story of her pet dog, Duke. Her father, Magloire, was quite an adept dog trainer. Her small, black and white, bulls-eyed dog was the marvel of the neighborhood. As Magloire visited the neighborhood in his horse-drawn wagon selling butter and eggs, the children would gather to watch Duke perform his greatest feat, a backward somersault done on the back of the horse. Word spread, and soon a vaudeville troupe on its occasional visit to the area, approached my grandfather. The $100 the manager offered was surely too tempting to resist with such a large family. Sometime later, the new owner was in town once again. He was ill advised in inviting my grandfather to see Duke on stage. As Duke was about to perform his "piece de resistance," Grandpere let out a whistle. Duke, with no further encouragement needed, leaped from the horse's back right into my grandfather's arms. The family's foray into show business was short lived.

GRAND'MERE'S MEAT STUFFING FOR PUMPKIN OR TURKEY

3 lbs. hamburger (or 1/2 pork and 1/2 beef)
1 small onion, chopped fine

Cover with water. Add salt and pepper. Cook twenty minutes.
Add 6 potatoes, peeled and diced and dried on a towel. Cook again until potatoes are soft. With hand masher, mash the potatoes with the meat. Add three cups of dried bread, or crumbs or unsalted saltines. Mash again with hand masher.

Add:

1/2 tsp. cinnamon
1/2 tsp. mace
1/2 tsp. cloves, ground

This makes enough stuffing for a 15 lb. turkey.

Another serving suggestion:

Place stuffing in a hollowed-out pumpkin. Put top back on and bake in a 350° oven for 2-3 hours. It is done when skin becomes soft. Take from oven, remove top and spoon meat and pumpkin onto plate. Serve with baked or mashed potatoes.

Within one block of the site of the old train station in Lawrence, Massachusetts, where my relatives first arrived in America and faced the taunts of neighborhood kids as "greenhorns," stands an old cast-iron street clock. I like to imagine my father, Fernand, passing that clock each day, checking his watch as he went off to school and, later, his office, so close to his family's stepping stone to America. It is my hope to restore that old clock and dedicate it to the memory of the Bernardins and Blanchettes. Hopefully it will serve as an encouragement to today's newcomers, whose own lives must be filled with the uncertainty and dreams that all our ancestors faced.

INDEX TO RECIPES

INDEX TO ILLUSTRATIONS

28. *Dining Room at Ellis Island.* Library Of Congress.

29. *The Foreign Language Sign.* Courtesy of Cort Ancman.

Dining Room At Ellis Island. Courtesy on New York Public Library.

31. *Map of Ports of Departure.* By Claudia Carlson, NYC.

33. *Russian Emigrants Landing From The Tender At The Barge Office, New York.* Drawn by Mr. Julius M. Price, from THE ILLUSTRATED LONDON NEWS, March 6, 1892. Author's collection.

38. *Detained Immigrants On Ellis Island, New York Harbor.* Drawn by M. Colin, from HARPERS WEEKLY, 1893. Author's collection.

42. Detail from *Emigrants Arrival At Cork.-A Scene On The Quay.* From THE ILLUSTRATED LONDON NEWS, May 10, 1851. Author's collection.

51. *The President Harding.* Courtesy of the artist, Frank O. Braynard.

57. *Reading Letters From Friends.* From HARPER'S NEW MONTHLY MAGAZINE, 1871.

63. *The Emigrants.* Artist unknown, from THE ILLUSTRATED LONDON NEWS, 1852. Author's collection.

72. *Our New American Citizens.* Drawn by G. W. Peters, from HARPER'S WEEKLY, May 23, 1903. Author's collection.

79. See page 38.

84. *Meeting Of Friends.* See page 57.

94. *Railroad Office.* See page 57.

99. *Emigrant-Landing In New York.* Artist unknown, from HARPER'S WEEKLY, June 26, 1858. Author's collection.

106. *In Battery Park - In And Out Of Castle Garden.* Drawn by F. Barnard, from HARPER' WEEKLY, September 3, 1887. Author's collection.

111. *New York. - Welcome To The Land Of Freedom - An Ocean Steamer Passing The Statue Of Liberty : Scene On The Steerage Deck.* Drawn by staff artist, from FRANK LESLIE'S ILLUSTRATED NEWSPAPER, July 2, 1887. Author's collection.

119.   Author's collection.

127.   *M.S. Saturnia.* Courtesy of the artist, Frank O. Braynard.

129.   *Exiles From Russia-Their First Day In New York.* Drawn by S. F. Yeager, from HARPER'S WEEKLY, February 18, 1882. Author's collection.

134., 149., 153., See page 111.

139.   See page 99.

143.   See page 38.

157.   Detail: *A Future Citizen from The Stream Of Immigration-Scenes At Castle Garden.* Drawn by W. A Rogers. From HARPER'S WEEKLY, May 27, 1882.

165.   *The Philadelphia* (formerly the *City Of Paris*). Courtesy of the artist, Frank O. Braynard.

171.   *Emigrants Leaving Queenstown For New York.* Artist unknown, from HARPERS WEEKLY, September 26, 1874. Author's collection.

179.   *The Emigration Agents' Office. The Passage Money Paid.* From THE ILLUSTRATED LONDON NEWS, May 10, 1851. From the author's collection.

187.   *The Imperator (*later *The Berengaria).* Courtesy of the artist, Frank O'Braynard.

189.   *Norwegian Immigrants At Castle Garden.* Drawn by W. A. Rogers, from HARPER'S WEEKLY, circa 1887. Author's collection.

196.   Author's collection.

201.   See page 129.

206.   *A Mysterious Functionary.* See page 106.

217-19. *Immigrant Portraits.* Courtesy of the Robert Watchorn Collection, Watchorn Methodist Church, Alfreton, England.

220.   *Map of Upper New York Bay* by Claudia Carlson, NYC.

225., 226. *Map of Ellis Island* and *Floor Plans* by Pamela Blackwell, NYC.

ORDER FORM

Sold To: Ship To:

_____   _____

_____   _____

_____   _____

_____   _____

Phone: _____

BOOKS: $16.95 each, $3.00 postage/handling. 3 or more books to same address, $2.00 p/h each.

Qty	Total Price	NJ Sales Tax	P/H	Total

Credit Card: _____

Name on card:_____

Card #:_____

Signature_____

PHONE IN YOUR ORDER 24-HOURS: 1-800-362-2489

By mail: make checks payable to Richardson Specialties. Mail to P. O. 8030 Brik, NJ 08723. NJ residents please add applicable sales tax.

"Food and history combine in Ellis Island Cookbook..."
SAN DIEGO UNION

"Cookbook tale of American dream..."
PALM BEACH POST

"Ellis Island Immigrant Cookbook provides glimpse into our culinary past..."
MIDDLESEX NEWS

"Taste of old country passed down in families..."
HARTFORD COURANT

"A treasury of recipes from the melting-pot cooks..."
THE NEWS-TIMES

"Immigrant cookbook makes history, culture come alive..."
THE INDEPENDENT

"What is valuable and a joy to read are the stories of the hopeful newcomers who passed through Ellis Island..."
THE DAY

"Familiar recipes arrived with immigrants at Ellis Island..."
NAPLES DAILY NEWS

"Immigrants preserved culture with foods..."
RECORD-JOURNAL

"A look at our immigrant past through Ellis Island recipes..."
FLORIDA TODAY

"Old world flavors are immigrants' legacy to descendants..."
SAINT PAUL PIONEER PRESS

"For over a century, America's immigrants cherished family recipes as link to homeland..."
LAWRENCE EAGLE TRIBUNE

"A history of immigrants through their recipes..."
THE SUN